The Purple Nest

A Groundbreaking Remain-at-Home Care Model for Elders with Dementia

Lori Kunkel
Judy Schiller, MA
Brynne Hicks, MSW, LCSW

The Purple Nest: A Groundbreaking Remain-at-Home Care Model for Elders with Dementia
Published by The Purple Nest LLC

Copyright © 2024 by Brynne Hicks, MSW, LCSW, Judy Schiller, MA, Lori Kunkel
All rights reserved.

No part of this book may be reproduced in any form or by any mechanical means, including information storage and retrieval systems without permission in writing from the publisher/author, except by a reviewer who may quote passages in a review.

All images, logos, quotes, and trademarks included in this book are subject to use according to trademark and copyright laws of the United States of America.

ISBN: 979-8-9905807-0-1
FAMILY & RELATIONSHIPS / Eldercare

Cover and interior design by Victoria Wolf, wolfdesignandmarketing.com, copyright owned by The Purple Nest LLC.

This book is not intended as a substitute for the medical advice of physicians, legal advice of attorneys, or financial advice from CPAs/accountants. The reader should regularly consult a physician in matters relating to the elder person's health, particularly with respect to any symptoms that may require diagnosis or medical attention. Likewise, the reader should consult an attorney for legal matters, and consult a financial professional for financial advice.

Reasonable efforts have been made to publish reliable data and information, but the authors and publisher cannot assume responsibility for the validity of all materials or the consequences of their use.

All rights reserved by The Purple Nest LLC.

This handbook is dedicated to "Team P."

Contents

CHAPTER 1 INTRODUCTION   1

CHAPTER 2 OUR INSPIRATION: LUCY'S STORY   5

CHAPTER 3 PHASES OF CARE   11
- The FLSA 80/20 Companion Services Exemption 12
- Phase One: Bringing in Part-Time Help 13
- Phase Two: Hiring Full-Time, In-Home Care 14
- Preparing for Around-the-Clock Care 15
- Cost of Hiring Companions 16
- Phase Three: Managing Increased Needs 17
- Phase Four: Leaving Home 19

CHAPTER 4 BRANCH ONE: THE ELDER   21
- Regression and Childlike Behavior 22
- Challenges with Remembering 23
- Understanding Emotional Changes 25
- Pathways to Improving Communication 27
- Shadowing 29
- Inner Places of the Mind and Soul 30

CHAPTER 5 BRANCH TWO: THE FAMILY   33
- Health and Financial Powers of Attorney 34
- Holding On to Independence 36
- Writing the Home Care Companion Handbook and Addendum 37
- Setting Up the Purple Nest Home Care Model 38
- Possible Scenarios for 24/7 Care 41
- Cost of Care Table 43
- Family Checklist 45

Chapter 6   Branch Three: The Companion 49

- A Day in the Life of a Companion 50
- Activities at Home 52
- Keeping the Elder Safe 53
- Handling Emergency Situations 55
- How to Talk to a Person with Dementia 57
- Practicing Good Hygiene 57
- Practicing Oral Hygiene 60
- Incontinence 61
- Managing Sundowning 63
- Making and Keeping Schedules for the Elder 64
- Companions' Work Schedules and Shift Crossovers 67
- Communication and Reporting 69
- Housecleaning and Being a Team Player 70
- Fulfillment and Rewards 72
- A Note about Boundaries 74
- Companion Checklist 75

CHAPTER 7   BRANCH FOUR: THE CARE MANAGER   79

- Finding a Care Manager 80
- Tasks Performed by a Care Manager 81
- Medical-Care Management 81
- Home-Care Management 84
- Ongoing Management of Companions 87
- The Cost of Hiring a Care Manager 90
- The Care Manager in a Legal Guardian Role 91
- Care Manager Checklist 92

Chapter 8 Branch Five: The Daily Money Manager **95**
    Finding a Daily Money Manager 96
    The Daily Money Manager's Task Details 96
    The Cost of Hiring a Daily Money Manager 101
    DMM Checklist 103

CHAPTER 9   EQUIPPING THE HOME   107
    Alarms, Locks, ID Bracelets, and "Sunflowers"................................. 107
    The Nitty-Gritty on Gates 109
    "Baby" Monitors...109
    Floor Alarm Pads and Motion Sensor Alarms 110
    Handrails and Anti-Slip Treads 110
    Helpful Kitchen Items 110
    A Few Final Recommendations 111

CHAPTER 10   COMMON BEHAVIORS OF PEOPLE WITH DEMENTIA   113
    Hiding and Hoarding 114
    Hallucinations, Delusions, Illusions, and Delirium............................ 116
    Sleep Issues and Sundowning... 118
    Aggressive Behaviors 120
    Sexual Behaviors..121
    Logging Behaviors Daily 122
    Addressing Behaviors with Medications 122
    Supplements, Diet, and Other Natural Approaches........................123
    Living with the Challenges 123

CHAPTER 11   CONCLUSION   125

ABOUT THE AUTHORS   127

ADDITIONAL RESOURCES   131

CHAPTER 1
Introducing a Proven Model for Remain-at-Home Elder Care

If your family member has dementia, it can be heartbreaking to watch them slip away as the disease progresses. Everyone wants their loved one to be happy and well cared for, but many families do not have the ability to provide all the care themselves. However, at some point the family is faced with possibly uprooting their relative and either finding a facility or bringing them to live in their own home, largely to keep them safe. We at The Purple Nest recognize these challenges.

We wrote this handbook to help the elder and their family create a remain-at-home care solution, so the elder can stay in the home they have lived in—perhaps for decades—and the family can continue providing support while maintaining their separate lifestyle.

As a training and consulting company, we provide step-by-step guidance throughout the care process to help the family smoothly implement a care solution and navigate any snags that might occur. Furthermore, this handbook outlines how to educate and build a team around the individual, so both the elder and their family have the support they need.

We developed the Purple Nest Home Care Model to aid those caring for an elder who is still able to do most of their own personal care. These tasks include eating, bathing, toileting, dressing, transferring (for example, moving from a bed to a wheel chair), ambulation (which means walking), and basic communication

NOTES

skills. Elders may need instructions and someone to "stand by," but otherwise they are able to perform these basic activities of daily living (ADLs). Although they are capable of doing these activities, they need companionship, partly to keep them safe, but more importantly to give them a higher quality of life, even as their cognition declines.

Many individuals are capable of performing ADLs and are not suffering from a type of dementia, and their family can implement this care model for them as well. This could include people who are living alone and would feel safer with a team of companions staying with them—part-time or even full-time—to keep them company, as well as help keeping up the home.

Another scenario could be a couple in advanced age (perhaps your parents or grandparents) where one spouse has dementia and the other does not. This situation can be incredibly demanding for the spouse who has become the caregiver. You could also put the Purple Nest Home Care Model in place for a person who has a terminal illness, to aid them during their final months or years.

The key criterion for using the Purple Nest Home Care Model is that the person's needs can be met *without* significant professional caregiving or conditions that require special equipment for lifting. For this reason, the members of the home care team are referred to as *companions* rather than *caregivers* (although companions do perform some tasks that fall under the caregiving role). When needed, however, this model can be modified by bringing in additional professional help to work in tandem with the home care team, which is discussed in Chapter 3: Phases of Care.

The Purple Nest Home Care Model recognizes that elders who suffer from memory issues are an ever-growing demographic in our society. According to an article on the Alzheimer's Association website called, "Alzheimer's Facts and Figures," in 2023 approximately 6.7 million people in the United States were living with Alzheimer's disease, which was projected to increase significantly by 2050.

People with dementia can usually continue enjoying activities for many years, such as dining out, going to the movies and public parks, attending church, and visiting friends—anything the elder is interested in doing. They may need prompts or reassurance but are able to follow instructions and can interact appropriately with others in public. If an elder tends to exhibit inappropriate behaviors, then the activities will be more limited. Participation in some activities may be at a slightly lower energy level, or some activities may need to be replaced with new ones, but most people in the early- to mid-stages of dementia are quite able to keep doing the activities they love to do.

One of the most beneficial aspects of this in-home care model is that the elder is able to remain in their own home, and they have the same three to four people staying with them all the time. This is far more settling and comforting as opposed to an agency where the elder might have three different caregivers per 24-hour period and the potential for high turnover of companions. Imagine the stress of dealing with a revolving door of new people coming into their home—and their life!

In the Purple Nest Home Care Model, this consistent team of companions, working together, gets to know the elder and their needs really well. The detailed records the companions keep can also make a difference in how health care providers approach treatment. Most of all, a consistent, dedicated team can bring a high quality of life to the elder, which also contributes to a higher quality of life for their family.

The three authors of this handbook were all members of a team that cared for a woman whom we call Lucy. Her story is told in detail in Chapter 2: Our Inspiration: Lucy's Story. Judy Schiller first saw the potential for creating a set team who would care for Lucy in her home. While managing Lucy's finances as her daily money manager and seeing the need for personal care, Judy created this care model. Judy and the family brought in Brynne Hicks, a licensed clinical social worker backed by twenty years of care management experience, as Lucy's care manager, which involved coordinating all her medical care. The family hired Lori Kunkel as a companion for Lucy, who worked for her for nearly three years.

These three women saw clearly that Lucy was receiving superior care and thriving and happy in her own home. This experience, coupled with this care team's experience and expertise in other caregiving situations, fueled a vision to bring this proven care model to others.

Purple is the color used to represent Alzheimer's disease, and it was Lucy's favorite color (as well as the color of Lucy's house), so we decided to name the business The Purple Nest.

The nest in the logo symbolizes the creation of a "home" (versus only sharing a "house"). A safe, welcoming nest/home is founded by five strong "branches": the elder, the family, the companions, the care manager, and the daily money manager.

The intent of the Purple Nest Home Care Model is to help families who have an elder with dementia create a safe and nurturing environment that can serve the elder for as long as possible in the home in which they feel best living. This handbook does not attempt to be an all-encompassing narrative for taking care of a person with dementia; many great books have already been written that dig deeply into the nuances and treatments of dementia. The Resources page on our website, www.ThePurpleNest.net, contains links to several books we recommend to those caring for a person with dementia, as well as to some of the products we refer to throughout this handbook. Assuredly, many more excellent resources also exist.

This book is deliberately called a handbook; it is designed to be a reference guide. It contains a great deal of information to digest, and you may find it at times somewhat overwhelming to read. Therefore, we suggest that you first read it to gain a general overview of the care model and then return to specific chapters to dig into the details as needed. Additionally, we have laid out this book to give you room to write notes in the margins.

Furthermore, we designed this handbook to accompany our online Printable Documents, which you can download free with the purchase of this handbook. These documents are great tools to create and maintain the home business and the overall care plan for the elder. You will also find training videos and webinars on our website. See the Resources page at the end of this book for instructions to access these materials from our website at www.ThePurpleNest.net.

We realize information can change rapidly, so we will address updates in laws and research in future editions of this handbook, on our website, and in our webinars. Feel free to reach out to us through our website's Contact Us page if you wish to bring something to our attention that seems amiss or important for us to be aware of—and, of course, if you have any questions that we can answer for you.

This handbook strives to describe the condition of an elder living with dementia and define the roles of the five main branches of this model. Furthermore, this handbook describes what can be expected overall in caring for a person with dementia in their own home. The Purple Nest Home Care Model has the potential to make an elder's waning years the highest quality possible. We hope you find this handbook helpful, if not transformative!

CHAPTER 2
Our Inspiration: Lucy's Story

This is the story of how one family and their team were able to create a unique home care scenario through trial, discovery, and no small amount of tenacity for a wonderful woman we will call Lucy. For privacy, the elder's name has been changed.

Lucy spent most of her adult life caring for others. She was a social worker and helped many people deal with trauma through her compassion and willingness to listen to people's stories. She was also a wife (widowed), mother, and grandmother. When she became ill, her daughter and granddaughter lived about three hours away, so extra help was required to care for Lucy and her estate.

Both of Lucy's parents and one of her two brothers had Alzheimer's disease. While her parents lived into their eighties, her brother died from the disease in his late seventies. Lucy's onset happened around age sixty-five, and she passed away just shy of her seventy-sixth birthday.

Lucy lived in an older two-story home that she and her late husband had spent many years lovingly fixing up. They had moved into it over thirty years ago, so the house—and neighborhood as well—were filled with many wonderful memories for Lucy. In addition to their home, Lucy and her husband invested in rental properties. After Lucy's husband passed suddenly, keeping up with the properties became too much of a task for her. To make matters worse, she was also challenged in the business aspects of landlordship, such as bookkeeping, paying bills, and collecting rents.

NOTES

With help from her daughter, Lucy finally hired a company that helps people regain control of their financial situation. It was through this daily money management company that Lucy met Judy. Initially, the company's owner and Judy thought they were being hired to help straighten out back taxes. However, as they dug deeper for answers and solutions, it became obvious that Lucy needed much more help.

Lucy was still making decisions, giving her opinions on matters, and voicing requests, but as time went on, those decisions and requests became less and less sound. One of the most challenging situations for the company was Lucy's initial refusal to let the company inform her daughter of the various decisions she was making. Since the initial contract was with Lucy alone, the company had to honor her wishes. After a couple of years, as Lucy's cognitive challenges increased, she finally began allowing her daughter into her financial and business worlds.

This was a welcome turning point for Judy, who by this time had taken over all of Lucy's many business needs. Judy was managing the numerous repairs at Lucy's rentals, clearing out storage units, managing the repairs on the home Lucy lived in, and paying all her bills, to name a few of the wide-ranging tasks.

As Judy took on more of Lucy's business dealings, she was in for some big surprises, such as discovering numerous stashes of cash around the home from tenants' rental payments. Plus, they began stuffing large amounts of cash into Lucy's unlocked mailbox after becoming frustrated that she would rarely cash their checks, which would get lost, used as bookmarkers, or end up in random drawers throughout the house. Judy finally had to knock on every tenant's door to determine who actually lived in each unit, because the leases had expired with little to no documentation in recent years.

At this time, Lucy began visiting a nice tenant of hers, named Mary, to have tea with as often as three times a day. (Lucy walked to Mary's home so often, because she had forgotten that she had already been to her apartment earlier that day.) Thus, Judy enlisted Mary as an independent contractor to be Lucy's first companion. Since Mary was newly self-employed and her business was still growing, she was excited to be paid to have tea with Lucy, as well as to take her to appointments, go on regular walks together, and run errands for Lucy.

Lucy originally had two roommates, which helped her feel safer in her home, but they were not always there. Initially, Judy hired other companions on a part-time, independent-contractor basis, and they would pick the days and hours of the week that worked best for them during the times that Lucy was home alone, that is, without the company of her roommates. When the roommates planned a month-long vacation, to avoid having Lucy be alone all hours of every day, Judy reached out to a close friend, a retired nurse, who was able to come and stay almost 24/7 during that month. It became clear that Lucy needed—and was adjusting well—to having more extensive companionship and care.

With the knowledge that Lucy required more scheduled time with companions, it became clear that Judy would have to assign companions to certain dates and times to facilitate Lucy's best care. Judy was aware that the companions were now being legally treated as employees and no longer as independent contractors, per employment laws. Thus, she enlisted the aid of a payroll company, and it was through them that she learned about the Fair Labor Standards Act (FLSA) 80/20 rule, which is critical to the implementation of the Purple Nest Home Care Model. (You will read a full description of this rule in Chapter 3: Phases of Care.)

The family initially suggested working with a care agency to provide 24/7 care for Lucy. Judy and the family continued discussing how to make the transition from part-time to full-time companionship/care for Lucy to best meet her needs. Also, as Lucy's daughter suggested, Judy located a care manager, Brynne Hicks, for Lucy's family to hire, which also took some of the heavy workload off Judy. Brynne immediately began coordinating all of Lucy's health care appointments, taking medical notes, tracking her medications, and so forth.

At the beginning of the care journey with Lucy, Judy found a reputable, affordable agency and began a "hybrid" model: using an agency for part of the time and independent companions for the rest of the time when the roommates were absent. However, the challenges with the agency began almost immediately. Several had scheduling constraints, the staff were almost always new with varying levels of training and experience, and since they changed shifts every eight hours, this exacerbated Lucy's confusion. The agency employees learned that the independently contracted companions earned more than they did, and some of them wanted to quit the agency and be hired directly by Lucy's family, which was a violation of their agency employment contract.

A best-case scenario began to form in Judy's mind. Could there be a way to *only* hire independent companions to work directly for Lucy instead of using an agency? Could the FLSA 80/20 rule be used to bypass agencies completely in order to create a better care model for Lucy?

Lucy's family initially preferred transitioning to only using an agency because of its perceived ease and to avoid pursuing a new business model, but Judy believed that transitioning solely to hiring independent companions as permanent employees would, ultimately, lead to better care for Lucy.

The roommates eventually moved out, and over the next few months Judy was able to fully develop the Purple Nest Home Care Model. Working with the family, Brynne, and the first 24-hour companion team, Judy's best-case scenario proved that her hunch was correct. Lucy's quality of life increased greatly, and she gained a stability she had not experienced for several years. In fact, since all the companions were women, she rather thought she lived in a sorority! Despite the complexities surrounding the development of the care model, everyone—especially the family—was happy with the outcome. It was a great comfort that Lucy was never alone and always engaged with someone whose focus was solely on her.

From the companions' perspectives, it was unanimous that they were caring for someone very special. The dementia had not lessened Lucy's humanity, her spirituality, or her sense of humor. Lucy had always taken excellent care of herself and was capable of participating in the activities she loved most, such as yoga, qigong, drum circles, a singing group, church, long walks, and much more. Before the COVID-19 pandemic, the companions regularly took her to movies and restaurants, as well as an occasional concert. While it was a perk to have their tickets paid for, the companions found it most rewarding to experience Lucy's joy! Close bonds were, indeed, formed in a short amount of time.

A typical day for Lucy might start with quiet time, such as a meditation utilizing a nature video with soft music on YouTube. (The companions also used this resource when Lucy displayed anxiety.) After a leisurely breakfast, if the weather permitted, the companion and Lucy might go for a walk through the neighborhood or drive to a favorite park to walk. If the timing was right, they might stop at a restaurant for lunch before returning home.

During the COVID-19 pandemic, finding activities to do at home became necessary. Staying in and not having friends come over was distressing for Lucy, so it was imperative to keep her engaged as much as possible. Doing things like playing brain/memory challenging games (of which there are many), reading aloud (which Lucy especially enjoyed at night as a bedtime routine), and coloring with pencils in adult coloring books were common. During the summer months there was a small vegetable garden in the backyard, and while Lucy might not have dug in the dirt, she enjoyed sitting on the deck in the shade and just listening to the birds sing. A lovely bird bath and a wide array of flowers brought birds to the backyard in abundance.

Lucy was also quite capable of helping in the kitchen. With supervision from the companions, she would chop vegetables, stir the food, read recipes, wash pans, and load and unload the dishwasher. She also enjoyed participating in folding and putting away laundry. Since each companion came and went every two to three days, they had to make and unmake their bed each time, and Lucy was always keen on helping with this task. She benefited greatly from feeling useful and involved.

In the evenings Lucy and the companions would watch television together. Shift change (when one companion left and another arrived) was at 7:00 p.m., so watching TV would usually occur after the departing companion had gone. This was a great time to have a small bowl of ice cream or other dessert, and it was a good way for both Lucy and the companion who was starting her shift to ease into the "nest" together.

Overall, the companions avoided letting Lucy watch too much television in favor of more mind-stimulating activities (although TV can provide focus and is not necessarily discouraged). Lucy would watch movies with subtitles even during the middle stages of Alzheimer's disease. Her responses to the programs proved that she was comprehending and keeping up quite well with the subtitles.

Sometimes the companions would put on YouTube videos of hymns with the lyrics displayed. Lucy had grown up in the church because her father was a minister, so she knew numerous hymns by heart and could sing along even without the words. However, the words on the screen activated Lucy's American Sign Language skills. It was beautiful to watch her sign to the music; it was almost a kind of dance! Hymns were also the most effective "funk buster," as one companion put it, which means they could shift Lucy from a sour mood into a good mood better than just about anything else.

The bedtime routine consisted of Lucy and the companion brushing their teeth together, getting into their pajamas, and, finally, Lucy reading aloud for fifteen to twenty minutes. Later, as the cognitive issues advanced, the companions read to Lucy, and then eventually the reading ritual was dropped altogether as Lucy became frail and lacked the energy and even the interest. By then, she seemed to just want to get under the covers and go to sleep.

A funny story happened one night while Lucy and a companion were brushing their teeth. The bathroom had two sinks, and a tiny elephant figurine was perched on the windowsill. Lucy suddenly took the little elephant off the windowsill and put it on the edge of the companion's sink. The companion quipped, "So, you want to talk about the elephant in the room, do you?" Lucy nodded her head, and they both cracked up with toothpaste foaming in their mouths!

Another illustration of her keen sense of humor was when Lucy answered the phone one time, and the caller asked for Dick. "No," Lucy said calmly, "We have no

NOTES

dicks in this house." Lucy and her companion absolutely howled with laughter! That sense of humor endeared Lucy to everyone who knew her. It was interesting that this part of her brain remained active well into the middle and even into the later stages of dementia.

Lucy loved to go for drives in the car. She would read road signs and the signs on businesses along the way. Often, she said she recognized a certain person standing on a corner and would say, "He's there every time I go by here." Sometimes she would make up stories about that person, quite elaborate stories at that.

When she saw tents of homeless people along the side of the highway her response was often, "Where are their parents? Do they know their children are living like this?" On stormy nights, sometimes Lucy would think of them and voice her concern for their well-being.

She hated violence of any kind, even on television. Just a simple fist fight would bring the retort, "Oh stop it now, you guys! Come on!" These are just a few examples of Lucy's humanity.

While Lucy also exhibited most of the behaviors associated with dementia, including "child-like" behavior at times, her companions always treated her as an equal and a friend. Researchers now believe that many dementia patients are cognizant of what is happening to them to an extent, and their so-called childish behavior is more about frustration over not being able to express themselves, rather than reverting to childhood. We learned from Lucy that it is vital for companions to remain respectful, as well as patient. It is important to remember that there is a person inside who has a whole life's story, and that it is a privilege for the family, friends, and companions to be a part of the elder's final chapter.

One companion said it this way, "When I tell people I take care of a woman with dementia in her home, a lot of times they say, 'Oh wow, that's a tough job!' I always respond by telling them, 'It really isn't what you would think. Lucy is an intelligent, lovely person and an absolute hoot!'" Hopefully, her story will inspire people to be more open and understanding when it comes to people living with dementia, especially because many, like Lucy, have brilliant minds that are being degraded by a disease we currently have no cure for.

CHAPTER 3
Phases of Care

The Purple Nest Home Care Model addresses four common stages of dementia care: bringing in part-time help; hiring full-time, in-home care; managing the elder's increased needs; and moving the individual to an outside facility. However, while this model covers these stages of care, it does not mean that everyone will ultimately require all four stages of care or use these methods exactly as described. You are always encouraged to do what works best for your elder and your family's needs.

In this care model, the companions actually work *for the elder or the elder's family*, rather than for an agency, potentially staying in the elder's home for 24-hour shifts, usually two to three days in a row (48 to 72 hours at a time). Therefore, a business must be set up by or for the elder. The companions spend the majority of their time during waking hours (usually a 16-hour period) on companionship activities versus caregiving activities. Also, the companions sleep in the elder's home during the same hours that the elder is sleeping.

An important aspect of this care model is the difference between companionship and caregiving—the difference is surprisingly meaningful in terms of activities, responsibilities, and how the US employment laws view these two roles. Briefly, the companion's main responsibility is to offer companionship and, as noted earlier, "stand by" while the elder performs activities of daily living (ADLs). The caregiver's responsibilities include physically helping the elder with ADLs, such as bathing, dressing, toileting, and feeding. The following paragraphs address why this distinction is so important, along with the US Labor Department's definitions of companionship and caregiving.

The FLSA 80/20 Companion Services Exemption Explained

The 80/20 ratio of companionship versus caregiving—referred to throughout this handbook as the *FLSA 80/20 rule*—is essential for this model, because it is due to this rule that our model is one third the cost of a home care agency. This rule, part of the Fair Labor Standards Act (FLSA), is referred to as the Companion Services Exemption and is federally administered by the US Department of Labor. This model also relies on fewer companions, providing more consistent care.

The FLSA 80/20 rule dictates that a companion must spend at least 80 percent of their awake working hours on activities engaged in "companionship" and no more than 20 percent of their awake working hours on activities engaged in "caregiving." The rule applies to how much companionship versus caregiving is conducted over the work week rather than during a 24-hour period. When this rule is followed, the law overrides the requirement to pay a minimum hourly wage and overtime wages and, instead, allows the family to pay a shift rate. Also, while a few states require an employer to pay overtime after eight hours in one day, most require overtime pay after 40 hours in a week. (To check your state's overtime rules, see the Resources page on our website for a link to research the overtime rule by state.)

The FLSA 80/20 rule defines *companionship* as "fellowship and protection," which is to "engage the person in social, physical, and mental activities, such as conversation, reading, games, crafts, accompanying the person on walks, on errands, to appointments, or to social events." The provision of "protection" means "to be present with the person in their home, or to accompany the person when outside of the home, and to monitor the person's safety and well-being."

The FLSA 80/20 rule defines *caregiving* activities as "assisting the person with ADLs, as well as meal preparation, driving, light housework, managing finances, assisting with the physical taking of medications, and arranging medical care." (You can find full details of the FSLA 80/20 rule at: www.dol.gov/agencies/whd/fact-sheets/79a-flsa-companionship.)

As we noted at the beginning of this chapter, the Purple Nest Home Care Model addresses four common stages of dementia care: bringing in part-time help; hiring full-time, in-home care; managing the elder's increased needs; and moving the individual to an outside facility. Let's take a closer look at each phase of care.

Phase One: Bringing in Part-Time Help

In the early stages of dementia, the elder may only need a companion to come in a few hours a week or perhaps a few hours a day. Hiring a part-time companion can be a good way to ease an individual into being helped, especially people who are fiercely independent. A companion might start out accompanying or driving them to an outing, such as a movie or a play that's showing in the evening. Other activities could include going for a walk in a park or participating in an exercise class. Driving at night or longer distances often becomes daunting as one ages; thus, reintroducing a favorite activity from the past could encourage the elder to step out of their current set of activities if they have become more housebound due to the disease.

This can reawaken a zest for life as well as a sense of regaining their independence, because the elder is doing something they love again, albeit with another person. In one example, a companion took Lucy to a performance by a South African choir. Lucy really loved the music, partly because she had spent time in South Africa during her college studies. This outing had such a big impact on her that she talked about it for several weeks.

The part-time companion could also take the elder to appointments, grocery shopping, or other errands. Having someone come in and clean the house is often a good way to introduce help. Allowing a gradual increase in the activities the elder does with a companion can provide a path of least resistance. Families should also consider people already within the individual's circle who are in good health and may want to make some extra money. Ideally, they would also be candidates for the 24/7 care team in the future (described in Phase Two below). If they are not, then it would be advisable to hire companions from outside the elder's circle and begin introducing them into the individual's life as soon as signs for the need to bring in extra companionship begin to emerge.

Numerous websites exist where companions advertise their services as independent contractors. Agencies can also provide companionship services, but the companions referred by an agency may not ultimately become privately hired companions for the elder, as those who work for agencies usually have noncompete clauses. As with any job some folks may not work out, which is OK since not all personalities mesh. The objectives during this part-time phase are twofold: first, to alleviate the time the family must commit to caring for or watching over their family member and, second, and perhaps more importantly, to get the elder used to someone else coming into their circle and helping them with their needs. During this phase, the companions bill the family/elder as independent contractors. (The Purple

Nest is not an agency or registry, but we have supplied several recommendations on where to find prospective companions on the Resources page on our website, www.ThePurpleNest.net.)

Phase Two: Hiring Full-Time, In-Home Care

How long it takes to reach this phase of care is not predictable, but the signs that it has arrived will be fairly apparent. Staying alone at night can become scary for some people with dementia, especially if they are beginning to experience hallucinations or delusions. These developments do not necessarily mean the elder must be moved into a facility for a higher level of care, as these behaviors can come and go at any stage of the disease.

Key signs that the elder is ready for full-time care include confusion around taking medications, wandering, losing their car, forgetting to pay bills, and, worst-case scenario, starting a fire in the home related to cooking or leaving a candle unattended. Be aware that urinary tract infections (UTIs), other infections, or a medication reaction can also cause hallucinations or delusions and various other behaviors in persons with dementia. These situations are often treatable and transient. It is, however, important that everyone around the elder is trained in how to identify the causes and how to deal with these behaviors. (We cover these topics in more detail in Chapter 10: Common Behaviors of People with Dementia.)

Whatever incidents trigger the realization the elder can no longer be left alone, it will behoove the family to be as prepared as possible ahead of time. This means completing items on the Family Checklist even while the individual is receiving part-time care during Phase One. (You can find the Family Checklist in Chapter 5.)

During this phase we recommend consulting with a business or elder law attorney to determine the best type of business classification to choose, such as a sole proprietorship or a corporation, such as an LLC. The attorney should consider the individual's estate and how their heirs may be impacted by business ownership. Before reaching the stage of hiring companions 24/7, it is imperative to have the business created in order to be compliant regarding payroll taxes.

When establishing the business to care for your elder, know that you can call the Department of Labor in the state in which the elder lives to discuss the FLSA 80/20 rule as it relates to elder care. Explain the business model you are creating as outlined in this handbook. Clarify any questions you may have regarding the FLSA 80/20 rule and ask if they see any challenges that could potentially lead to complaints by the companions to the Department of Labor and how you could prevent these challenges.

Preparing for Around-the-Clock Care

Before a team of companions can begin staying overnight, you need to prepare a bedroom for them. It should be a comfortable and welcoming space, as getting good rest is essential for a companion to provide great care. A companion will be spending 24 to 72 hours at a time in the home, which means they will be there day and night for one to three days. Getting a good night's sleep, as well as having a place of respite, is a must!

Each companion will require their own set of sheets and perhaps pillows and blankets, as everyone has different needs. Some companions may bring their own pillows or a favorite blanket but be prepared to purchase some of these items. It is essential to have a dresser large enough to supply a drawer for each companion, so they do not have to bring everything every time they come to stay. Plus, they can store their bedsheets and towels in the dresser to avoid laundering every time they stay. (How to set up the companions' room is detailed on the Family Checklist in Chapter 5.)

Once the elder requires 24/7 care for the entire week, we recommend hiring three main companions, plus a fourth who can be brought in one to four days per month as required, which could cover anything from illness of one of the companions to filling in holes in the schedule to filling in for vacation days. This number of companions works well in the Purple Nest Home Care Model, but you can change the care team's structure to fit the needs of the individual elder and the family's needs.

Of course, a family member can be a member of the care team. Having a family member isn't necessary to provide stability to the team, but it can potentially save money. Plus, being involved in the elder's care a few days a month may be within their bandwidth, whereas living together full time is a much larger commitment. Familiar, happy faces can make a world of difference to the elder's comfort level.

Make sure you or a cleaning crew does an initial deep cleaning of the elder's home before bringing in the new team. Additionally, hiring a cleaning service to clean the house at least once a month is a good idea, so the companions can easily maintain the 80/20 rule. (Remember that light housekeeping falls under the 80/20 rule's definition of caregiving, not companionship.) Perhaps a friend of the family would be interested in this task, or a companion could come in on an hourly basis during a day off.

Preparing the home for 24/7 companionship is also a good time to get general home maintenance up to par with tasks like duct cleaning (including the dryer), furnace maintenance, roof and gutter cleaning, and chimney sweeping if applicable. Once you have set up accommodations for the companions, the team can be brought in to stay around-the-clock, seven days a week.

As the case may be, determine if the elder's pet(s) can or should remain in the home now that companions will be staying there. Allergies are always a possibility, so if the pet is critical to the well-being of the individual, include this detail when running ads and interviewing candidates. Additionally, make sure the pets are up to date on their vaccinations, grooming, pet supplies, and so forth. Include the relevant phone numbers (for example, vet, groomer, and dog walker) on the list of other important phone numbers in the Addendum, which is a document that is attached to the Home Care Companion Handbook. Both documents are created by the home care team, namely the family and care manager, and are essential for the care of the elder. (See Chapter 5 for more details.)

Cost of Hiring Companions

In the Purple Nest Home Care Model shifts are scheduled as 24 hours, usually two days in a row, though sometimes a shift may be just one day and sometimes more than two days. This is up to the team and the person who is supervising the scheduling. When it comes to deciding on the wages for 24-hour care, you will want to take several points into consideration. Despite the fact that the FLSA 80/20 rule allows you to pay less than minimum wage and no overtime, we strongly suggest you start with the minimum hourly wage for your state or region within the state (some states have varying minimum wages). Since the companion is paid hourly even while they are asleep minimum wage becomes a good starting point. However, if the family is able to increase the wage, particularly considering inflation levels and the desire to secure quality companions, it will behoove them to do so. This could be done gradually as well, particularly if great companions become part of the team, and you want to retain them. Note that a companion who works just nine to ten shifts per month can pick up part-time work with other clients who may require only a few hours a week.

In Lucy's case, some companions had other clients they billed separately on a contract basis (as in Phase One), while other companions were retired or semiretired and satisfied with this compensation. If one or more of the companions on the team has other part-time clients, their outside commitments will have to be factored into the scheduling. (See the Phase Two Sample Schedule on the Printable Documents page on our website.)

Phase Three: Managing Increased Needs

As dementia progresses to the middle and late stages of the disease, the needs of the elder will increase. The elder will no longer be able to perform activities of daily living (ADLs) as independently as before. Their behavior will begin to change and become more challenging at times (the degree depends on the individual). Incontinence may become more frequent; confusion, delusions, and hallucinations can increase; and the elder may become frailer physically. At this stage, some patients become uncooperative, belligerent, sexually inappropriate, and even combative.

If the elder's behavior is still manageable, albeit more challenging, consider these questions:

1. Can the elder remain safe in the home?

2. Can the companions remain safe in the home?

3. Which ADLs have become impossible for the elder to do?

4. Is the elder still sleeping through the night?

5. Do the companions have the skill sets to care for the elder at this stage or do you need to hire more skilled or credentialed caregivers?

6. Is additional training available for the companions?

7. Does the family need to hire professionals, such as nurses, physical therapists, occupational therapists, or CNAs to come in a few times a week to help with some tasks?

8. If the home has two stories and the sleeping accommodations are upstairs, can everyone—including the companions—move to the main floor comfortably?

NOTES

9. How important is it to everyone involved to keep the person at home?

10. Will remaining in the home provide the highest level of care and quality of life for the elder?

11. Do you need to make changes to the home regarding accessibility (for example, coming in and out of the house with a wheelchair)?

12. What are the costs of making the changes?

If the family or health care representative decides to meet the challenges of keeping the elder at home, then you must implement one important change as soon as possible: amending the pay structure for the companions. Once the scales have tipped toward more than 20 percent caregiving, the business needs to switch to paying an hourly wage (instead of a 24-hour shift rate), according to the FLSA 80/20 rule, and begin paying minimum wage and overtime according to the laws of the state in which the elder resides. As mentioned previously, it is important to know the specific rules in the elder's state. (See the Resources page on our website for a link to research the overtime rule by state.) For this reason, the companions are now referred to as *caregivers* in this phase of care, as they are working in a caregiving capacity.

One scenario to keep the wage expenses comparable to the full-time, in-home care provided by companions in Phase Two is to have a four-person team where three of the caregivers work the same two-day shift every week, and the fourth person comes in on the seventh day. In this scenario, each of the three caregivers is paid eight hours of overtime per week, while the fourth person is not paid any overtime. (See the Phase Three Sample Schedule on the Printable Documents page on our website.)

What can happen when your family member's dementia has reached the more advanced stages, though, is burnout for the caregivers. Even though they are sleeping at the elder's home, the days can be long with a person who has become uncooperative, progressively confused, and generally more difficult. At this stage, the elder's incontinence could increase, which, in turn, requires paying more attention to the elder's personal hygiene and more laundering. If the caregivers are now helping with other ADLs, such as dressing and bathing, the day can become exhausting. Working (awake) hours could be as many as ten to sixteen hours, which is a long day. Often, people with middle- to late-stage dementia no longer sleep through the night, so sleep for the companions becomes interrupted as well.

To break up the 24 hours of care into more manageable shifts, the scheduling becomes more complex. The shifts can be roughly broken up as follows: a day shift from 9:00 a.m. to 4:00 p.m. and a night shift from 4:00 p.m. to 9:00 a.m. If the elder is sleeping or in bed from, for example, 10:00 p.m. until 8:00 a.m., then each shift is working with the individual seven waking hours. You could divide the hours of work while the elder is awake in other ways as well, but at this point it likely would require having at least five people on the team. The overtime incurred will push up the cost as well.

During this phase, the big question that comes to the front and center is, "What is the elder's quality of life like now?" If the elder is still engaging with those around them, is aware of their surroundings, and displays joy and well-being, then it certainly may be worth the extra efforts and costs to keep them in their home.

During the later stages of the disease, it can be difficult for the family to determine if and when to move the elder to a facility. Statistics show that late-stage dementia such as Alzheimer's disease can last 1.5 to 2.5 years, so perhaps every month the time can be extended to stay in their own home is a top priority. These are questions only the family or health care representative can answer. That said, if the finances exist and the training level of the caregivers is adequate, dementia patients can remain at home until the end of their lives.

Phase Four: Leaving Home

In many cases, this is the time when the person with dementia needs to be placed in an environment where they can get around-the-clock skilled care, especially with the complexity of scheduling the companions and the expense of hiring more skilled personnel. Most states offer private group homes, also called adult foster care homes or board and care homes, which generally house four to six elders and can provide this type of care. Memory care facilities offer around-the-clock care as well. The cost of these facilities varies widely, as does the quality of the facilities. We recommend using a placement specialist. These professionals offer their services for free and thoroughly vet the recommendations they provide. (We have provided links to a few companies on the Resources page on our website.)

This can be a tough transition for the elder and the caregivers as well. They may have been sharing the home with the elder for years and developed a strong

NOTES

bond. Also, the change can be unexpected due to a fall or other health emergency, which means the individual is leaving their home abruptly, and the caregivers are now suddenly unemployed.

Often, the individual will do better if they are placed in the new home and given a chance to settle in before people they know visit, such as the companions/caregivers. It may depend more on the wishes of those running the facility, but if the elder is distraught the companions/caregivers should be allowed to visit. Another option to consider is offering to pay the companions/caregivers to visit the elder at their new location a couple of times a week on a contract basis for a while. Also, an occasional get-together with everyone (the family and companions/caregivers) can be a nice way to help the elder feel secure and loved.

Taking cues from the elder and the companions who have come to know them so well can make this phase easier to cope with. As always, providing the highest quality of life possible for the elder is the key consideration throughout all four stages of care. Dementia is a tough disease to predict and increasingly hard to manage as time goes on. At The Purple Nest, our wish is for the best journey possible for each elder, their family, and everyone in their circle of support.

CHAPTER 4
Branch One: The Elder

The elder is the foundation of every aspect of the Purple Nest Home Care Model. We like to think of the home as a nest, interwoven with five crucial "branches." The branches of this nest (and our home care model) are the elder (the first and most important branch), the family, the companions, the care manager, and the daily money manager. These branches are an integral part of the nest; they weave themselves into the fabric of the system that keeps the elder safe and secure in their own home. Above all, the home should be filled with love, compassion, understanding, and dedication. In this chapter, the intention is to bring a greater understanding of the elder's experience as they live through the debilitating progression of dementia.

Perhaps the most important point to keep in mind when dealing with a person with dementia is that the disease is slowly but surely taking over their brain's ability to function properly. Biologically, the disease is making structural and chemical changes in the person's brain. Many families report personality changes in their family member or behaviors never displayed before. Symptoms can begin showing up in various ways, such as a person who is normally easygoing and cheerful becoming angry, depressed, and distrustful. However, not every individual with dementia will display all the behaviors associated with dementia; plus, each type of dementia can produce different behaviors.

Changes in the elder can be gradual and result in misreading what is going on with them. Some negative behaviors come off as deliberate or willful but are more likely to be frustration due to the lack of control the elder is experiencing. The individual realizes they are not able to do things or remember things as they used to, which can be quite confusing and even frightening, thus causing unusual and sometimes disturbing behaviors. The elder may feel embarrassed or foolish, because they fail at some simple task they have done for most of their life. Changes in the brain can lead to changes in the personality that can be positive or negative. Some people with dementia are reported to have become "nicer" overall than before the disease and others "grumpier."

Our brain cells perform thousands of tasks every day, most of which we are not even aware of. In a person with dementia, cells are being damaged in a random manner, often causing their behavior to be unpredictable. Therefore, the individual may be able to do some things and not others, and this won't make sense to those around them. For instance, people with dementia can often remember things from the distant past in detail but not what they did yesterday or an hour ago.

Also, due to the disease, the elder may "receive" a message quite differently than how it was "delivered" or intended, causing confusion for both people in the conversation. This might happen when delivering more complex instructions to the elder, whose ability to learn has become more challenged due to the progression of the disease. The individual may be trying as hard as they can, but if frustration sets in, the behavior may become abrasive. It's important to understand that they are not trying to "act out"; they simply cannot grasp something both parties think they should be able to grasp, especially since they could in the past. Also, trying to force the elder to learn something new can bring on obstinance.

Regression and Childlike Behavior

It is a popular misconception that people with dementia revert to childhood and eventually display only childlike behaviors. This is an oversimplification of a complex situation. You can read a helpful article on the Elder Law of East Tennessee website, titled "People with Dementia Aren't Children—So Don't Treat Them That Way." This article gives a well-rounded explanation of what the brain of a person with dementia is going through as it responds to the disease. Several behaviors come across as childish, such as tantrums, irrationality, forgetfulness, and vocabulary problems, but it's important not to let these occurrences cause the home care team to treat the elder like a child. Doing so may exacerbate the behavior rather than improve it.

The article points out that, to understand these behaviors, one could conceptualize the brain of the individual with dementia as a computer whose data is being deleted a little bit at a time. There is usually no single setback in cognitive decline, but rather the elder is continually experiencing setbacks, because the information being deleted expands further and further. For instance, "home" will often become where they grew up as a child rather than the home they live in currently. They may even forget that their parents, spouse, or other family members have passed away and say they need to call or visit them, or they expect their deceased relative to come home. Lucy experienced this quite often, ever increasingly with the onset of the later stages.

One's first reaction to an elder who talks as if their deceased family members are still living may be to correct them, as this is obviously an alternate reality in which they are living, but that is not the recommended method.

The number-one rule in dealing with an elder with dementia is to *never argue with them*. Arguing with a person who has no recollection of just having been told something three times will only aggravate both people in the discussion. While the elder will rapidly forget the details of what's been said, they may hold on to the feeling they got from the conversation, which can make them hold on to any resentment that accompanied the exchange. Imagine the elder has just been reminded that their parents are dead. They will more likely hang on to the part of the conversation with the bad news that their relatives are no longer alive as opposed to recalling what the argument was about.

Likewise, using childish language when speaking to the elder may bring unwelcome responses. It is best not to use words like *diaper* and *potty* but rather *underwear* or *protective underwear* and *bathroom*. Watching your tone when addressing an elder with dementia is also important. Most people know when they are being spoken to in a condescending tone. Rather than treating the elder like a belligerent child, if there is an argumentative situation, a better choice would be to distract them and redirect the conversation to a different topic or even to simply step into another room. If possible, leading the individual to an outdoor space can be a pleasant form of distraction and redirection.

Challenges with Remembering

When speaking to a person with dementia, it can be tempting to ask them if they remember something or someone. Asking about a memory they cannot recall can cause frustration, even if unintentional. It's better to describe a memory to the elder. For example, if a friend is coming over, it's fine to tell the elder about the last time the friend visited and that they went to the botanical gardens and had a great time.

NOTES

Retelling the story will avoid putting the elder on the spot to remember, potentially causing embarrassment, and simultaneously getting them excited about the upcoming visit.

You can use several helpful mindfulness techniques with people who have memory issues, because many of our everyday conversations are either about things that happened in the past or about things that will happen in the future. There's a tendency to want to ask our elders questions about their distant past, which is something people in early and middle stages of the disease might enjoy talking about. However, elders with dementia will not be able to remember what they did yesterday, last week, or probably last year. Therefore, talking about the recent past should be off limits. Likewise, talking about the near future such as, "Oh, your daughter is visiting this weekend," can backfire. In many cases, you will quickly realize that this is a mistake, as many elders may hang on to this kind of information and begin asking over and over, "When is my daughter visiting?" This can cause them undue anxiety.

Alternatively, working with a person with dementia is a great opportunity to focus on the present. Slow down and tune into what they are experiencing right now. What kinds of objects do they see? What sounds do they hear? Do they smell something yummy being cooked in the kitchen? How does the outside air feel on their skin? Living in the moment is a great practice for all of us.

Even the most familiar things in an elder's life can become foreign to them when the brain isn't connecting the dots. There were times when Lucy would suddenly declare she did not know where she was, even though she was in her own home. Sometimes this happened when walking in the door from being outside or returning from another room in the house. With a frightened look on her face, she would ask whose house she was in. An effective answer was, "You are in your home, safe and sound" and reciting the address. It seemed the familiar address resonated the most and calmed her down quickly. Her brain could not register what she was seeing with her own eyes, but she could recall the address from the recesses of her mind. Fortunately, in Lucy's case this incident happened only sporadically. However, in the later stages of the disease she often asked to go "home," which to her was where she grew up with her parents. Generally, one of the best responses to challenging dementia behaviors is to reassure the individual that *they are safe.*

Understanding Emotional Changes

Emotional outbursts or overreactions can be signs that the elder is overwhelmed, maybe due to too much stimuli or being asked to do too many things at once. Their behavior may appear as though something dramatic or violent is happening even though it isn't. Something is usually causing these outbursts, and looking for the triggers when they happen can help prevent them from reoccurring.

Some basic triggers that can bring on these types of reactions are:

- Being required to think about several things at once (like all the steps involved in taking a shower)

- Not understanding the directions being given to them

- Being tired or not feeling well

- Being in pain

- Being treated or spoken to like a child

- Trying—or being asked—to do things they can no longer do

- Not being able to make themselves understood

- Feeling inadequate

- The attitude of the companion/caregiver—rushing the elder or displaying frustration with them

When an elder has an outburst, this is an example of the type of information and data the companions should collect and record in the daily progress notes. Eventually, the patterns will emerge and give the home care team the opportunity to shift the behavior by avoiding the triggers. Lucy could get upset (though usually mildly) by just being given a choice between two things, such as, "Would you like

NOTES

spaghetti or baked chicken for dinner?" It was ultimately better to simply tell her what was for dinner and, if she turned her nose up at it, to offer the alternative. Interestingly, this aversion to making a decision became less of an issue for Lucy during the later stages of the disease. For Lucy, other behaviors also shifted in a positive direction throughout the years with the disease, so be encouraged that an unpleasant pattern may change and that the companions and family can have an influence.

If an elder's behavior is extreme and ongoing and nothing has helped, medications might help. Unfortunately, most medications that are meant to curb aggression can cause unwanted side effects, such as drowsiness, balance issues, and slowed movement and thinking. Widely used medications exist that are specific to dementia, such as Aricept, which can slow the disease and help with moods, agitation, and other behavioral issues. The medical team in charge of the elder's treatment plan should discuss medications and make recommendations, but it is always prudent to become as informed as possible before making decisions concerning medications. Of course, every individual will have to test what works best for them, and it may take some time to find the right solution. Meanwhile, finding effective behavior modification methods may solve many of the issues the elder and the home care team are facing.

Often an activity may upset the elder, and they may need to stop for a moment to adjust or catch up to what is being asked of them. They may require a simple explanation of what is happening—even if it's something they've done hundreds of times before. This could include tasks they do on their own, like brushing their teeth, or something that involves more steps and other people. For instance, if the elder is getting a haircut but the stylist or barber is unaware that they should be explaining what they are doing, the whole experience can suddenly become a fiasco. The solution is two-fold: find a salon or barbershop with sympathetic staff and explain to the stylist or barber beforehand what the elder needs to feel safe and calm. When the care team finds a good fit, make this the elder's regular salon or barbershop. Some stylists specialize in hair care for people with dementia, and some will come to the home to give the elder a haircut or style. If haircuts are particularly difficult for the individual, it's worth doing an online search for someone with this specific service.

Pathways to Improving Communication

Communication barriers are among the most important things to understand when interacting with people with dementia, especially as the disease progresses. The elder's inability to make themself understood can cause a lot of frustration for everyone, but none more so than for the elder themself. Imagine knowing in your own mind what you want to say—perhaps something common or simple—but you cannot make the words come out of your mouth. This is what a person, particularly with some kinds of dementia, such as Alzheimer's disease, may deal with at all times, especially in the later stages of the disease.

Family or caregivers trying to communicate with the elder may think it's best to let them "exercise" their brains and come up with what they are trying to say on their own. It's OK to help the elder find the word or words they are searching for unless it upsets the individual. Sometimes it will be obvious what the elder is trying to say, other times not. By taking cues from what the individual is able to say, along with the circumstances, it is often fairly easy to figure out what they are trying to communicate. Otherwise, try asking simple questions or have the elder point to the object, person, or room. Above all, stay patient and calm, and if they cannot make progress, find a way to drop the question before the elder becomes upset. Sometimes just saying something like, "I'm not sure, but I'll look into it," can make them feel like they've succeeded in being understood. Of course, if the person is in pain or discomfort, the companion or caregiver must make more effort to understand as fully as possible what is happening.

During the middle stage of the disease, Lucy increasingly found it hard to express what she wanted to say or ask. However, she could still respond appropriately to what was being said to her. In the later stages of the disease, she was often unable to respond at all, and when she did try to speak, it would sometimes come out as gibberish. This is a tough point to reach, especially for the elder's family members, as this is where they may feel they have lost the individual to the disease. Language and communication are so central to us as human beings that the loss of effective communication is a key reason dementia is such a cruel condition for the people living with it, on both sides of the relationship.

NOTES

Here are some simple ways to improve *verbal* communication with a person who has dementia:

- Speak softly and slowly, waiting for a response before repeating, without repeating too many times.

- Eliminate distracting noises or having too many sounds happening at one time, like a TV and multiple conversations in the room.

- Use short and simple sentences or questions that address one thing at a time.

- Ask yes/no questions.

- Use hand gestures to help explain what you are conveying.

Nonverbal communication is equally important and sometimes more easily understood by both parties. This can also mean the elder will pick up on the emotions of the person they are with. If a family member or a companion/caregiver is feeling some kind of angst in, perhaps, a challenging situation with the elder, this angst often exacerbates the situation. It is best to keep a calm exterior no matter how upset you might be on the inside. What we do with our hands, faces, and bodies communicates more than we are aware of to others around us, and this is particularly important to keep in mind when working with a person who has dementia, because they are highly attuned to nonverbal cues. This can also be a valuable tool. Using nonverbal forms of communication, such as pointing or gesturing can help get a point across to an elder with dementia and vice versa.

As dementia advances, it becomes increasingly important to "read" whether the elder is feeling ill or in pain. If the disease has rendered them unable to verbally tell the caregiver what is happening in their body, nonverbal communication is all that remains. If the elder is in extreme pain, that will likely be obvious; however, it's best to avoid getting to this point by identifying the source of the pain before it becomes extreme. Other signs like increased agitation can indicate pain. Again, asking short, simple questions (such as yes/no questions) will help you get to the bottom of a problem. Go slowly and take a break if you aren't making progress. The more relaxed a person with dementia is, the better the chance of success is—with nearly everything—not only with communication challenges. If verbalizing is not an option, the caregiver needs to do some detective work based more on circumstances than on words.

Here are some simple ways to improve *nonverbal* communication with a person who has dementia:

- Make eye contact while speaking to them.

- Remain calm and pleasant.

- Show affection with gentle touches and strokes, perhaps on the arms or shoulders.

- Demonstrate the action or task you are asking them to perform.

Shadowing

It is common for a person with dementia to follow their companion everywhere they go. This is referred to as *shadowing* and is a sign of insecurity or that the elder is feeling confused about where they are. The person they are following around appears to be in complete control, so "sticking with them" makes the elder feel more secure. Another possibility is that the elder is bored. Whichever the case, this can be annoying for the person being followed, especially when it continues for hours. The worst reaction would be to snap at the elder and demand they stop the behavior. That will make them feel more insecure, which will likely make the situation worse. Instead, giving the elder something to do can often help ease both scenarios.

A few ideas to keep the individual occupied are giving them a basket of laundry to fold, having them sit at the table to color with their favorite music playing, or having them sit with their "rummaging box" in front of them. (You will learn more about these distraction techniques and other ideas in Chapter 10: Common

NOTES

Behaviors of People with Dementia.) They may fold and refold the laundry. It's OK to bring them clean laundry that has already been put away, if need be, as long as they are content and feeling secure. Any "chores" the elder can participate in will also give them a sense of achievement and belonging.

Sometimes the elder will feel frightened if they cannot see their caregiver, and they believe they are alone. For a time, Lucy would get agitated if the companion was not in her line of sight. This made the companions feel like they couldn't even go to the bathroom without causing Lucy distress. It seemed that the instant Lucy could not see anyone else, she believed she was alone in the house. A couple of things worked well to alleviate Lucy's fears. One was to always tell her where the companion was going and how long she would be gone. The other was to write the information on a small erasable board that was placed right in front of Lucy that said something like, "I'm going to the bathroom; I'll be right back." Because verbal instructions can be lost almost instantaneously with people with dementia, written communication can be a more effective method to keep them reassured, as long as the elder is able to read.

At night Lucy's companions would put a sign on the outside of their bedroom door that said, "Sally is here with you. We are getting up at 8:00 a.m. Please go back to bed." The companion could put a similarly worded sign on the inside of the elder's door to discourage them from leaving their room. However, if the elder usually gets up in the night to use the bathroom (and a portable commode is not in their room), this sign might send them back to bed before relieving themself, so this needs to be taken into consideration.

Inner Places of the Mind and Soul

When it comes to understanding what is happening with someone who has dementia, it can be easy to make assumptions based on their everyday behaviors. Realizing that their brains are not functioning properly is important to remember, but it is also important to keep in mind that portions are still intact, and the elder's life lessons can serve those around them. There may be nuggets of wisdom still waiting to come out, if only someone would tap into them. One time a companion was telling Lucy about a dream she'd had. In the dream the companion was riding her bicycle, and the road in front of her began rising until it was almost vertical. She peddled as hard as she could and was feeling like she would not be able to reach the top before falling helplessly backward. The companion thought it was a nonsensical dream, but Lucy said, "No, you are struggling with something in your life, and you don't feel like you are in control of it." The companion was immediately able to identify the struggle. These little nuggets of wisdom came out on many occasions with Lucy, particularly if she was asked the right questions.

Spirituality is another dimension that those around a person with dementia might tend to forget about. Those deeper places in the human spirit may remain unscathed by the disease that is attacking the physical part so aggressively. Helping the elder stay in contact with their spiritual path can bring them much-needed peace and security. If the individual attends a place of worship, keep going for as long as possible. The other members of the congregation should know about the elder's dementia, and while most will figure it out over time, at some point you may want to share the information, so everyone can adjust to the changes in the elder's behavior.

Many places of worship offer online services. This can be a way for the elder to stay in contact with their spiritual beliefs if they can no longer physically attend. In Lucy's case, the companions made sure she was able to tune in to her online church service on Sundays.

While dementia certainly changes people in all sorts of ways, some more than others, it is important to always remember who they are inside and try to find little ways of helping that person remain present. Above all, keep showing them a lot of love through patience, touch, kindness, and reassurance. There will be good days and not-so-good days, and yes, sometimes bad days, but in the end, knowing that everything that could be done for the elder was done can give the family and everyone on the home care team a treasured feeling of comfort and peace.

CHAPTER 5
Branch Two: The Family

As mentioned, we like to think of the home as a nest, interwoven with five crucial "branches." The branches of this nest (and the Purple Nest Home Care Model) consist of the elder, the family, the companions, the care manager, and the daily money manager. In this care model, the family members who are finding their way through the challenges of caring for their family member who has been diagnosed with some type of dementia are the most important participants of the care team. As the dementia symptoms become clearer and more pronounced, frequently during the latter part of the early stage, the reality begins to set in that significant changes in the elder's lifestyle—as well as the family's lifestyle—are going to have to be made. It is a sad and often devastating reality that few families are prepared to address.

This handbook shows families an alternative to moving their elder out of their home while giving them an extremely high level of care and quality of life and even possibly extending their life expectancy. The Purple Nest Home Care Model guides families in setting up a system that allows the elder to remain in their own home for as long as possible. What we learned from working with Lucy and others inspired us to bring this proven care model to the broader population, and we sincerely hope this model helps your family's situation.

Many details need to be sorted through and considered when a family begins assessing the options and various models for caring for their family member. The standard care models include moving the elder to an assisted living or memory care community, hiring an agency to look after the elder in their own home, having the elder live with a family member, or having a family member move in with the elder.

The Purple Nest Home Care Model allows the elder to remain in their own home while being cared for by companions rather than by the family or an agency. No matter which model the elder and the family choose, significant changes to everyone's lives ensue. We wrote this handbook to help the elder and their family set up a home care team that eases the impact of these changes.

Determining where the elder will live requires careful and thorough thought. Ideally, when selecting a care model for the elder, the family can agree on the priorities and weigh all the factors, such as the pros and cons, costs, location of each care model, the recommendation of health care providers, and most importantly, the wishes of the person with dementia. Calling a meeting of all parties who will be directly involved in the decisions surrounding the care of the elder is a great place to start. Collectively deciding on the best care model for the elder requires diligence, commitment, cooperation, and patience.

While the Purple Nest Home Care Model is mainly geared toward people with dementia, this care model—based on 80 percent companionship and 20 percent caregiving—could be used for someone with another disease, such as the early stage of cancer or even for an elder who is becoming frail enough that living alone has become a concern. In our direct experience, for elders who are still able to perform activities of daily living (ADLs), this model can work very well for them. As the elder requires more caregiving, particularly in managing ADLs, they will have to change the model of care.

Health and Financial Powers of Attorney

The first step, if not done previously, is to gain health and financial powers of attorney for the elder. You must address these steps while the elder can still show they are cognizant of what they are signing. Usually, no matter who participates in this legal process, the elder must be of "sound mind" to complete the paperwork. The family may need several legal documents to fully care for the elder and their assets; therefore, we suggest two designees are selected where applicable.

Here is a brief overview of these documents:

- The health care power of attorney (HPOA) designates another person to make medical care decisions on their behalf.

- Whereas the HPOA allows a person to make health care decisions for another person, a durable power of attorney (DPOA) allows one to make financial decisions on another's behalf. It is important to complete these documents while the elder is still able to understand what they are signing.

- The advance directive is a document where an individual records their wishes for the end of life, thereby giving guidance to their agent. Sometimes called a living will, this document is most often completed when someone is in good health but looking to the future.

Several helpful resources exist to complete this important paperwork, such as estate attorneys, elder law attorneys, and family law attorneys. That said, in many states a lawyer is not required to complete this paperwork; you can simply complete a standard form and have it notarized (if notarization is required by the state the elder lives in). It is a good idea to contact all institutions in which the person has money to see if they accept a DPOA. Overall, getting professional legal advice is the most thorough and safest way to handle this process, as any "do-it-yourself" documents can occasionally mask abuse or significant family conflict.

In the event these important documents have not been completed before the elder is too confused to understand them, the family should consult with an elder law attorney about securing guardianship and conservatorship of their elder, so they can make and execute decisions for their family member. When a person is unable to do so themselves, a guardian is a court-appointed person to make *medical* decisions, and a conservator is a court-appointed person to make *financial* decisions.

Holding On to Independence

Many seniors in the United States live independently in their own homes, sometimes after they have lost a spouse and find that they need to become even more independent now that they are "flying solo." According to an article by Harvard University's Joint Center for Housing Studies, titled "The Number of People Living Alone in Their Eighties and Nineties Is Set to Soar," it is projected that by 2038, the number of households with one person aged eighty and over and living alone will reach 17.5 million, more than double the 8.1 million recorded in 2018.

You may be all too familiar with this scenario, or you may be looking for a solution for an older married couple (perhaps your parents or grandparents), particularly if one spouse has dementia and the other is acting as a caregiver. At an advanced age, it can be incredibly demanding for the spouse who has become the caregiver. The spouse or family can implement the Purple Nest Home Care Model for this scenario as well.

The sense of losing one's independence can be the hardest obstacle to overcome, whether care is needed for a couple or a single elder. When it comes to discussing a change in an elder's living situation, it can be akin to "walking on glass." Often it takes incidences like a fire in the kitchen, losing one's car repeatedly, or forgetting to pay bills and suddenly having the electricity or water turned off to bring the person into the reality that they are no longer able to completely take care of themself. At this point family members are forced to start having tough conversations with their elder, who may resist giving up control of their finances or health decisions.

In Lucy's case, she was more willing at first to relinquish control of her finances to a daily money manager than to a family member. Eventually she became comfortable having a care manager arrange medical appointments for her, as well as keep track of medications and all personal medical data. (You can read a full description of what each of these professionals does in their respective chapters.) While Lucy's daughter did have full powers of attorney (the HPOA and DPOA), Lucy was not originally open to relinquishing control until she reached a point of just not wanting to be bothered with the details anymore. Once Lucy was ready to relinquish control, she could then just relax and enjoy life.

Having these two essential documents in the hands of the adult child (or children) does not mean they can immediately make decisions for their parents; that control depends on the capacity of the elder to make decisions.

Bringing in professionals can be a great help when trying to convince a fiercely independent person to give up some part of their "power." The professional will not have the history a family member has with their elder—and, honestly, often that history may have been challenging at times. Hiring professionals like a care manager and daily money manager are added expenses, but they provide a strong foundation for the home care team and can take a huge load off the family's plate.

It is important that these two people have a good working relationship with clear roles and tasks. It is particularly helpful during the initial stage of putting the home care model into place and during the transition stage of moving from having a part-time companion (or companions) to hiring a team of companions for 24/7 care. The array of tasks these professionals take care of is significant, as outlined in their respective chapters.

Down the road, other trusted individuals in the circle of friends and family can take over some or all those duties, but having a care manager and daily money manager dial-in and fine-tune the care model can save the family time, headaches, and even money.

Writing the Home Care Companion Handbook and Addendum

The care manager can be a great help to the family by assisting with a particularly important task: writing the Home Care Companion Handbook, customized for the elder and family. This document details the wants and needs primarily of the elder, including listing and describing the elder's hobbies, interests, favorite places to visit (for example, parks, theaters, and restaurants), favorite music, dietary preferences and restrictions, and favorite recipes. This handbook can also include what the family is looking for in a companion, their expectations of the companion, and the best ways for the companion to interact with the elder. (See the Sample Interview Questions for Companion Position on the Printable Documents page on our website, www.ThePurpleNest.net.)

The care manager can also write a separate Addendum, which would include the pertinent health care contacts, emergency phone numbers, current medications, supplements, and so forth. Both documents will evolve over time, so do not stress over making them 100 percent complete right away, though the more information that can be given to the new care team in the beginning, the better. We recommend only sharing the family's Home Care Companion Handbook with prospective hires, and then sharing the Addendum after they are hired, so you do not share private health details and contact information with anyone who is not a member of the care team. (Refer to the Home Care Companion Handbook and Addendum templates on the Printable Documents page on our website.)

Even if the family hires a care manager, at no time is the family shut out of decision-making concerning the care of their family member. If the family has chosen to establish the business with themselves as the employer rather than the elder, they could be making many decisions on a regular basis, depending on how much of the day-to-day care and management they wish to handle. The family members can choose how much they want to be involved and how much they want to delegate.

That said, there is an alternative to being the party in charge when the elder and family cannot arrive at satisfactory agreements. If discord exists between the elder and the family and the elder does not have the capacity to make decisions, the family can choose to have a guardian and conservator appointed. This can remove a great deal of the burden on the family and even allow for a better relationship to be forged between parent and child (or other relatives, such as siblings). This is a potentially difficult and expensive legal process, so the family should consider this path carefully with the advice of an elder law attorney.

Setting Up the Purple Nest Home Care Model

As you will see on the Family Checklist at the end of this chapter, the family must complete many tasks in order to set up the Purple Nest Home Care Model to keep an elder in their own home. Even once everything is in place, the family will need to be available for decision-making in all sorts of scenarios. These might include medical treatments (perhaps considering alternative modalities or clinical trials), home upkeep and repairs, hiring or firing companions, the need or wish for the elder to take a long-distance trip, and the wide variety of things that can pop up in daily life for anyone. Caring for an elder's life can be something like a part-time job. In the home care model we set up for Lucy, the family spent about five hours per month on financial management and one to five hours on home care decisions. The management of the care team adds several more hours per month.

The financial cost of keeping an elder in their home is certainly one to be considered. While the best-case scenario may be to keep an elder in their own home, it is not financially viable for everyone. The Cost of Care Table in this chapter shows the differences in costs for full-time care to keep an elder at home provided by an agency versus the Purple Nest Home Care Model. While the Purple Nest Home Care Model costs significantly less than an agency for 24/7 care (approximately one-third the cost), your family may need to look into assisted living and memory care facilities as viable alternatives. Those care options cost less than the Purple Nest

Home Care Model in most cases, so depending on the elder's finances, it is worth making the comparisons.

A working family member might be able to take advantage of the Family Medical Leave Act (FMLA) for up to twelve weeks per year (if their employer is eligible) to set up the Purple Nest Home Care Model. Also, if the elder has a long-term care (LTC) insurance policy, it can be used to pay companion wages, though it might not cover the entire expense.

The following points detail the advantages of the Purple Nest Home Care Model of having a team of companions who work for and take care of an individual in their own home. When compared with agency staffing, the Purple Nest Home Care Model offers many advantages, such as significantly higher hourly wages for the companions (partly due to the companions being paid while sleeping during a 24-hour shift), which leads to a higher caliber of companion applicants. Also, the ability to offer companions a flexible work schedule. (On average, a companion has four days off at a stretch and, with additional planning, several more days in a row per month.)

The elder's home may be cleaner and better organized than when hiring an agency, because the companions live in the home part of the time, so they may take more ownership of its organization. After all, it is easier to tolerate a mess for only an 8-hour shift versus a 48- to 72-hour shift. For example, Lucy's house went through several rounds of clutter clearing, resulting in an overall improvement in the state of the home. (We suggest using a cleaning service at least once a month to ensure the companions do not exceed the 20 percent caregiving tasks. Remember, cleaning is considered a caregiving task, not a companion task, per the FLSA 80/20 rule.)

The following table lists out the greatest advantages of the Purple Nest Care Model.

- **The elder has fewer staff changes to deal with,** since the companions stay 24 to 48 hours (as opposed to only eight hours at a time).

- **The companions can provide better feedback** to the elder's medical team, because they are spending longer amounts of time with the elder.

- **The elder is consistently engaged one-on-one** with the companion—conversing, staying busy, getting exercise, and participating in other healthy activities.

- **This may ultimately lead to an increase in life expectancy** and help with cognition, as reported by an article from Johns Hopkins Medicine, titled "Dementia Care: Keeping Loved Ones Safe and Happy at Home." The research showed that when the right support is brought in and introduced as early as feasible, people with dementia can live at home longer and with a higher quality of life compared to those living at home without that support.

- **The companions are not caring for a different elder** (with different needs and different challenges) every day.

- **The companions develop a stronger, deeper relationship** with the elder due to the extended time together.

- **The companions have more personal input** in the daily running of the home.

- **The opportunity exists to create a stronger team dynamic,** because the team is small and consistent.

- **The companions can make a sustainable living** working eight to ten days a month (albeit in 24-hour shifts).

- **The companions are able to pick up other part-time work** if they choose to do so.

Possible Scenarios for 24/7 Care

When an elder requires 24-hour care, many types of care and options are available. These scenarios vary depending on the level of care needed and the budget. The options for 24-hour care include hiring care at home, either through an agency or privately, or moving the elder to a care facility. Depending on the individual's needs, the facilities that provide 24-hour care are assisted living, adult care home, residential care facility, memory care, and nursing home (also referred to as an intermediate care facility). Here is a brief description of each:

- **Assisted living:** Facilities are comprised of private apartments with provided meals, medication distribution, some additional care as needed, and 24-hour emergency services. This is the most independent care model on this list.

- **Adult care home:** Six or fewer residents live in a private home in a residential neighborhood. The elder generally has their own room and sometimes their own bathroom. At least one caregiver is available at all times. Note: Not all adult care homes offer 24-hour awake caregiving staff.

- **Residential care facility:** Six or more residents live in a home-like setting in a residential neighborhood. They have awake staff 24 hours a day.

- **Memory care:** Memory care facilities offer a locked setting with 24-hour awake care. Residents may have private or shared rooms.

- **Nursing home/intermediate care facility:** This is the highest level of care available for people with complex medical or social needs. These facilities have hospital-like settings with 24-hour nursing care available, including licensed nursing staff and certified aides.

The Cost of Care Table on the following pages compares the two key remain-at-home scenarios for 24/7 care: utilizing an agency versus hiring privately and implementing the Purple Nest Home Care Model. We encourage you to study this cost comparison carefully, because you may find that the Purple Nest's unique approach is best suited for the elder's needs as well as the family's financial situation. Keep in mind that this model is based on the FLSA 80/20 rule, which differentiates between companionship and caregiving. Importantly, this differentiation highly influences pay rates (for companions versus skilled caregivers), the shifts (8-hour shifts versus 24-hour shifts), and whether overtime pay is required.

If your loved one is going to be cared for at home, it is important to include in your budget the monthly bills of the home, such as the mortgage payment, utilities, yard maintenance, house-cleaning services, groceries, dining expenses, and so on. Usually, all these costs are factored into the total charges for the facilities listed above. They are not, however, included in the costs in Figure 1, which compares agencies versus The Purple Nest Home Care Model. For our sample we show the wages paid by both an agency and the Purple Nest Home Care Model in Portland, Oregon, in 2024. This is strictly meant to help make the comparison between the two models of care. (Note: In the Purple Nest Home Care Model, the companions work directly for the elder or the elder's family, not for The Purple Nest.)

COST OF CARE TABLE:
Comparing Two Remain-at Home Models for Elders with Dementia

Agency Home Care Model 24/7			
Description of Care Provided	**Description of Personnel**	**Average Cost per Day**	**Average Cost per Month**
Agency manages/controls the entire care process Entails having 2 – 3 different companions per 24-hour shift Often not the same companions every day High turnover of companions	Companions may be certified caregivers or noncertified employees $20 per hour is the average hourly wage Overtime pay after 40 hours = $30 per hour Caregivers earn 40% – 50% of the fee charged to client Caregivers are bonded and insured	$42 per hour average cost to the elder Total cost is $336 for an 8-hour shift 3 people per 24 hours = $1,008 Sometimes there is an additional charge for night shift *Note: Overtime is not figured into these totals.*	**Monthly Cost:** **$30,240 – $31,248** Companion Wages Only **NOTE:** agencies do not typically offer care management nor daily money management.
The Purple Nest Home Care Model 24/7			
Description of Care Provided	**Description of Personnel**	**Average Cost per Day**	**Average Cost per Month**
Elder/family manages the entire care process Care manager and daily money manager may join the team Companions work 24-hour shifts for the elder or family This model assumes 3 main companions plus 1 – 2 backups (consistent team members)	Companions can be friends, semiretired persons, or experienced caregivers 24-hour shift with no overtime pay or minimum wage requirements All terms of employment are controlled by the employer/employee	Companions start at $365 per 24-hour shift Averages to $15.20 per hour (about minimum wage) including while asleep *Note: The costs to hire a care manager and a daily money manager are not included in the right-hand column.*	**Monthly Cost:** **$10,950 – $11,315** Companion wages only ***A savings of $240,000 per year in this example!***

Figure 1. Cost of Care Table: Comparing Two Remain-at-Home Models for Elders with Dementia (all rates listed above are for Portland, Oregon, effective 2024; rates vary by state)

NOTES

The scenario not included in the table is when an elder requires more than 20 percent caregiving, which shifts the employees' status from companions to caregivers. This does not necessarily mean the elder must move out of their own home, but, per the FLSA 80/20 rule, the wage structure needs to change. The costs increase, and, quite possibly, the level of expertise of the caregivers may have to increase as well. It may be necessary to bring in more highly trained, certified professionals such as Certified Nursing Assistants (CNAs) and nurses. It may become challenging and more expensive to secure 24/7 care as people skilled in these professions can be in high demand and, therefore, not available.

One scenario would be to bring in professionals just for specific tasks such as bathing or medical needs outside the companions' skill set. In Lucy's case, occupational therapists, physical therapists, and home-visiting nurses came to the home for weekly visits on an as-needed basis. Also, there may be times when you need to call on an agency to offer supplementary care, so it is a good idea for families to at least have researched a reputable company. Examples of when you might need to use an agency include the sudden onset of a serious illness, injury, and surgery recovery where the elder might require around-the-clock, awake care for a short period of time. Companions would need night support to be able to sleep and rest, and an agency may be the best resource for providing overnight personnel.

When the elder reaches the point where they require significantly more professional care, such as the need to use equipment for bathing or the elder can no longer use the toilet, change out of soiled undergarments, or feed themself, it may be time to consider a facility. In the meantime, implementing this remain-at-home Purple Nest Home Care Model provides the elder with an extremely high quality of life. With the companions focusing on safety and bringing fullness to the elder's life, the family can have peace of mind and establish (or reestablish) a semblance of normalcy in their own lives.

Family Checklist

The following list of tasks may appear daunting, but these tasks do not need to be completed by the family alone. You may be able to assign tasks to a daily money manager, care manager, other family members, and friends. While the list can be completed in a different order than laid out here, we recommend getting the legal items rolling as soon as possible. The Family Checklist is a great organizational tool for tracking the progress of various processes and tasks. (See this checklist plus the more detailed, comprehensive Expanded Family Checklist in both PDF and Excel forms on the Printable Documents page on our website.)

We suggest dating each item as completed.

#		
1		Become the elder's power of attorney for both financial and health affairs (DPOA and HPOA).
2		Complete with the elder their advance directives as mentioned previously in this chapter.
3		Open a joint checking account with the elder.
4		Establish a business either in your name or the elder's name.
5		If you decide to do so, hire a daily money manager (DMM).
6		If you decide to do so, hire a care manager (CM).
7		Create a bill-paying system for the elder's household expenses (or assign this to the DMM).
8		Write or obtain a hiring contract for the companions or assign this to the DMM. (See the sample Home Care Companion Employment Agreement on our website's Printable Documents page.) Note: Be sure to have a lawyer who is licensed in the state in which the elder lives review the contract.
9		Consult with an insurance agent to obtain a worker's compensation policy for the business (or assign this to the DMM).

10		Consult with an insurance agent to determine if an Employer Non-Owned Liability (ENOL) auto policy is needed for added coverage on the companions' vehicles while they are driving the elder (or assign this to the DMM).
11		Create a shared Google (or other) calendar for everyone on the home care team (or assign this to the DMM or the CM).
12		Hire a house-cleaning service to clean the home at least once a month (or assign this to the DMM).
13		Hire a landscaping service to take care of the yard (or assign this to the DMM).
14		Provide a current, clear photograph of the elder for the home care team to give to emergency personnel in case the elder wanders.
15		Order a medical alert bracelet for the elder (or assign this to the CM).
16		Collect names, addresses, and phone numbers of neighbors who are willing to watch out for the elder in case they wander.
17		Complete the Home Care Companion Handbook. (Download the template from our website's Printable Documents page; the CM may help with this.)
18		Complete the Addendum to the Home Care Companion Handbook, which lists contact information for the family, CM, DMM, emergencies, doctors, dentists, and so forth. (Download the template from our website's Printable Documents page; the CM may help with this.)
19		Create a list of questions for hiring a companion. (Download the Sample Interview Questions for Companion Position from our website's Printable Documents page; the CM may help with this.)
20		Determine, with the CM, who will do the initial training of companions.
21		Create a General Home Management Task List for companions. (Download the template from our website's Printable Documents page; the CM may help with this.)

22		Create an End-of-Shift Checklist. (Download the sample from our website's Printable Documents page; the CM may help with this.)
23		Create an Emergency Packet. (Download the sample from our website's Printable Documents page; the CM may help with this.)
24		Prepare a bedroom in the elder's home that companions will use as their own.
25		Supply the companions' bedroom with adequate sets of sheets, blankets, pillows, and other necessary items.
26		Confirm the kitchen has all the basic supplies needed to easily prepare meals.
27		Confirm the washer and dryer and dishwasher are all in good working order.
28		Make (at least) two extra copies of the house key and purchase an outdoor lockbox to hold one copy. Add the lockbox combination to the Addendum.
29		Have all the main living spaces of the home deep-cleaned (ideally prior to hiring companions 24/7).
30		If the elder's pet(s) will remain in the home, make sure they are up to date on their vaccinations and examinations.
31		Inventory all valuables in the home and determine where best to keep them.

NOTES

CHAPTER 6
Branch Three: The Companion

Becoming a companion to a person with dementia can be an extremely rewarding experience. While it does not require any formal educational certification, it would be beneficial to have basic first aid and CPR training and possibly CNA training. Regardless, being a companion does call for a great deal of kindness, patience, and compassion. Every individual with dementia will be different, because they remain just that: an individual. Their personality may go through some changes, but inside resides the person they have always been. As it is with getting to know any older human being, the experience has great potential to reveal an extraordinary person who has done many different and interesting things during their lifetime. We are all the sum of our experiences, and helping a person with dementia live out their remaining days places a significant amount of responsibility in the hands of a companion. While this chapter is geared toward a 24/7 working scenario, much of the material is applicable to a companion who is employed on a part-time basis as well.

The most important point for the companion to keep in mind when entering the world of companionship with a dementia patient is that they are there to provide the highest quality of life possible as the individual lives out their last years. The companion is perhaps the most important member of the care team, as they spend the most time with the elder. As a reminder, the home care support team potentially consists of the primary family, a care manager (CM), a daily money manager (DMM), as well as companions and friends of the individual. The medical care team

NOTES

may consist of a general practitioner, neurologist, dentist, optometrist, audiologist, and a variety of other professionals who participate in the wellness management of the individual receiving care. No other participant spends as much focused time with the individual as the companion, at least once around-the-clock care is put into place.

In this remain-at-home care model, the people who enter the home of an elder with dementia may or may not be traditional caregivers, although the companions are there to lend a hand in the "care" of the elder. In order to work with a person who has dementia, one does not necessarily need to have professional experience. Anyone who has the temperament, desire to help, or perhaps has had prior experience with a family member or friend with dementia can make a great companion. A neighbor or friend of the elder can become a companion, or a retired person who is seeking part-time work can be a great fit. In most cases, the companions will not be familiar to the individual, but when possible it is advantageous to hire people with whom the elder is already familiar.

A Day in the Life of a Companion

As explained in Chapter 3: Phases of Care, the companion's role requires that at least 80 percent of their time is spent engaging in activities defined as "companionship" and no more than 20 percent in activities defined as "caregiving." The caregiving side of the equation is distinguished by the elder's ability to perform activities of daily living (ADLs). As mentioned, the elder may need instructions and someone to "stand by" as they bathe or dress, for example, but they are able to complete these tasks by themself or with limited assistance.

Other specific duties a companion may perform are driving the elder to the doctor or other appointments, running errands with the elder, helping the elder with their crafts or hobbies, and, most of all, offering conversation and meaningful connection. The companion is there to help the elder continue to enjoy the things they love doing for as long as possible.

To maintain the 80/20 ratio of companionship versus caregiving within a work week (or in the case of the Purple Nest Home Care Model, a two- to three-day shift), the FLSA rule states that the companion may perform no more than 20 percent of caregiving tasks in a workweek, not on a daily basis. Therefore, if a companion is working three days per week, then they must hold their caregiving tasks to not more than 20 percent of those three days.

Here is an example of caregiving tasks for a general daily guide:

- **Bathing/showering:** Sometimes bathing is an overwhelming task for the elderly. Many do not require daily bathing, as they perspire less, so every other day or every three days may be sufficient. Facilities usually bathe their patients twice a week, which would be about every three to four days. Helping the elder take a full shower, including washing and drying the hair and getting dressed, usually takes about 30 to 60 minutes.

- **Preparing meals:** Breakfast preparation usually takes about 15 to 20 minutes, lunch about 20 minutes, and dinner about 1 hour, for a total of around 1.5 to 1.75 hours per day. If it is in the budget, eating out or getting take-out food for one meal a day cuts this time down to .75 to 1.5 hours per day.

- **Light house cleaning:** This includes cleaning up after meals, laundry, sweeping or vacuuming, cleaning the bathroom, tidying things up, watering plants, and taking out the trash and recycling. This takes about .75 to 1.25 hours per day. (Note: Not all these tasks must be done daily).

- **Recording events and behaviors in the daily journal:** This task takes about 10 to 15 minutes per day.

These timelines are estimates only, as the needs of the individual and the setup of their home will vary. It is not necessary to keep track of every minute of every day, but it is good practice to get a sense of how much time, on average, the caregiving activities take during a shift. By doing so, the family or daily money manager can bring in additional help for such things as cleaning, showering once or twice a week, or prepared meals (for example, online ordering services that send several full meals at a time on a set schedule). This additional support will help everyone ensure compliance with the FLSA 80/20 rule. The companion's main focus should always be on companionship and keeping the elder focused and present in the moment.

Activities at Home

A companion engages with the individual in their home by doing things like reading, putting together simple puzzles, playing memory games (www.Alzstore.com has some great suggestions), looking at photo albums, putting together new photo albums or scrapbooks, creating arts and crafts, going for walks in the neighborhood, watching favorite television programs, arranging phone calls or FaceTime visits with family members and far-away friends, and planning visits with friends.

In particular, spending time creating and looking at photo albums and scrapbooks is a great way to keep a person with dementia in contact with their memories and the names of people from their present and past. It's a good idea to ask the family to provide some pictures that they might like to see put into new albums. Though the current way of keeping photos has been largely delegated to the cloud and other digital resources, having a physical book of favorite pictures can be a lasting treasure for the entire family. The companion can help the elder add colorful stickers, write brief captions and the names of people below their photos, and maybe even add whimsical comments to the pages, making it more fun while also recording some family history.

If the individual is interested in coloring or doing arts and crafts, the companion can facilitate several activities. Usually when we think of coloring, we envision the books of our childhood, but a wonderful variety of coloring books are designed specifically for adults. Rather than using crayons, we suggest colored pencils, as the elder may think they are being treated like a child when given crayons.

A great arts and crafts activity is making collages. Thumbing through magazines to find pictures, illustrations, and words can be exciting for the elder. Gluing those materials to a sheet of construction paper helps maintain dexterity skills (as does coloring and cutting). Collages are a free-flowing project, as opposed to precise, thus avoiding frustration if deftness is an issue for the elder. The individual may have craft projects they have long enjoyed, such as knitting, crocheting, or embroidering, so, of course, the companion should encourage them to continue these if the ability is still there.

The world of arts and crafts holds a vast number of choices, so figuring out what works best may take some trial and error. If a companion has a favorite craft or hobby and can facilitate teaching it, they can certainly give it a try, though it's usually best to keep simplicity in mind.

There may be a history of specific hobbies for an elder, such as woodworking or putting together model airplanes, weaving or sewing, creating tile mosaics, and so forth. These are more complex and may not be possible as the disease progresses. If being engaged in an activity becomes complicated and causes frustration or anxiety, this may indicate that the elder could have progressed beyond their ability to continue with that activity. On the other hand, perhaps the elder is OK doing this activity for a shorter time, maybe only 10 or 15 minutes. The companion can then put away the project and take it out again later.

If the person is unable to do the more advanced hobbies they once enjoyed, it may be best to store those items out of sight, so they don't constantly remind the elder of their inabilities. Also, it can be helpful to do certain activities consistently, at the same time and for the same amount of time, on a daily basis. (More is addressed concerning schedules later in this chapter.) Finding balance is most important, especially when trying to judge if an individual's capacity to continue doing something they love appears to be waning.

Overall, the companion's goal is to keep the person with dementia as focused and active throughout the day as their health conditions allow. Going for a walk in the neighborhood can be just as enjoyable as getting in the car and driving to a park or other destination and can help keep them tuned into their "home base" location. Try letting the elder lead the way to test their capacity to find their way home.

Keeping the Elder Safe

Keeping the elder safe in the home is covered in detail in Chapter 9: Equipping the Home, but a few items bear repeating here, as we cannot overstate the importance of safety. In particular, if roaming is an issue the companions must be diligent in setting the door alarms. When they go off, they are loud and will probably upset the elder for a while afterward. Putting up signs can curb the impulse to open the door. (See sample signs on the Printable Documents page on our website, www.ThePurpleNest.net.)

The companion should always have a current photo of the elder in their phone in case they need to call the police. Also, a wandering person with dementia should wear a medical alert bracelet with pertinent contact information on it. These bracelets are deliberately made to be difficult to remove, so they remain on the elder's

NOTES

wrist. The elder may resist wearing one at first, but usually gets used to it in time. If they don't wander, wearing a medical bracelet may not be necessary; it's ultimately up to the family or care manager to determine whether the elder needs to wear a medical bracelet. If neighbors are close by whom the individual knows, make sure they have the phone numbers of all the companions, in case the individual elopes to their home or if they happen to witness the elder wandering.

Baby monitors are another essential piece of equipment. We suggest using them at night, but depending on the elder, the layout of the home, and other unforeseen factors, they may be needed during the day as well. Using the baby monitor at night is important, as the companions must be able to hear if the elder gets up, calls out, or displays concerning breathing patterns, such as sleep apnea. If the elder snores loudly, the companion can turn down the volume or place the monitor away from their head to lessen the sound.

Some families install cameras in the rooms most used by an elder like a bedroom, and that is a fine option as well if everyone is agreeable to it. The companions should always be informed if cameras are in use in the home.

Navigating stairs can be an area of concern, especially if balance has become an issue. Balance problems can often be accompanied by muscle weakness. If possible, move the elder to a room where they will not have to use stairs. We advise that the care manager or the family ask the general practitioner for a home health evaluation, so a physical therapist can teach the companions how to safely navigate the stairs with the elder. If the companion needs to carry items up or down the stairs, they should do so on a separate trip without the elder.

Another safeguard, particularly at night, is the use of tall "pet gates," which are taller than child gates. These are useful in the hallway leading to the bedrooms, especially if they are upstairs. If the elder wanders at night, they might fall, so a barrier can give the companion a chance to get to the elder before they get too far. Weakness in the hands and dexterity can become a challenge with older dementia patients, so pet gates can be hard for them to open. If they are able to open the gate, then weaving a bicycle chain around the bottom rungs of the gate, locked with a padlock, can provide added security. That said, the companion on duty must be able to kick down the gate in case of an emergency.

If the gate doesn't stop the elder from going through, then it's best to put it away and try it later when the disease progresses to a point that the gate could be useful. A substitute could be an alarm pad on the floor at whatever point the elder needs to be stopped, perhaps in front of their bedroom door. Alarm pads are often used at the bedside as well to alert the companion if the elder is getting out of bed, but they are quite loud and may upset the individual more than they are helpful. A less alarming alternative is to place newspaper on the floor next to the bed. The sound of rustling paper can alert the companion that the elder is out of bed without scaring them. Motion detectors are another great solution. (See the links to these and other products on the Resources page on our website.)

Handling Emergency Situations

Although working as a companion does not require the skills of a professional, at least not during the first stages of the disease, the companions should have basic first aid and CPR training. If a companion has not taken these courses, it would behoove the family to invest in providing them for those caring for their elder. Making basic first aid and CPR training a prerequisite to the position might mean passing up a good employee.

The family could require companions to take another step further in their training with a course in becoming a certified nursing assistant (CNA). Some classes are available online, though this may differ from state to state. Advanced skills may come with a higher wage requirement, so the family should consider where their comfort level is, not just financially, but also the skill level they want from the companions. As the elder's dementia progresses, the family will need to seriously consider whether the companions need additional training.

Whether or not the companion has advanced training, they must have a clear understanding of what to do in an emergency. While calling 9-1-1 should be the first step in a real emergency, it's important for the family or care manager to provide additional guidance for these situations. (See the Emergency Actions section in the Home Care Companion Handbook template on the Printable Documents page on our website.)

For example, recommended emergency actions include:

1. Take a deep breath to remain calm.

2. Call 9-1-1.

3. Tell the operator there's an emergency.

4. Say your name, where you are, and provide the nearest cross street if possible.

5. Explain what happened.

6. Follow all the operator's instructions carefully. Do not hang up until told to.

7. Relay all health conditions or concerns of the elder to the EMTs, such as diabetes or other chronic conditions, medications the elder is on, and any allergies.

8. The companions should know whom to call after they've called 9-1-1. It may be the family, the care manager, or both, whoever is designated in the handbook.

9. Ask which hospital the EMTs intend to go to and provide them with your phone number in case they are rerouted to another hospital.

10. Follow safely behind the ambulance with important items (per the emergency packet in the Home Care Companion Handbook).

How to Talk to a Person with Dementia

While we covered this subject in The Elder chapter (Chapter 4), we want to reinforce some general suggestions that are good to follow regarding communication. First, it is important to never argue with a person who has dementia. Arguing, as well as correcting something the elder says, can perpetuate defensiveness in the individual, which can result in behaviors often thought to be childish (for example, tantrums, irrationality, and vocabulary problems). In turn, it is easy to then speak to the elder as though they were a child, but doing so will likely exacerbate the unwanted behavior rather than improve it.

The more the companion speaks to the elder as an equal in all matters, rather than as an authority figure, the better the results will be. That said, there may be times when the companion must take a stern stance if a behavior calls for it. In general, always strive to stay neutral on subjects that might upset the elder such as politics, religion, or highly opinionated topics. Keeping conversations on the lighter side helps control the overall mood in the home. Many people with dementia experience depression, and in those cases, it is even more important to avoid unproductive conversations that lead to arguments or deflation of self-esteem.

As mentioned earlier, do not ask a person with dementia to remember things in the near past, sometimes as recently as ten minutes ago. Many individuals do retain experiences and names from the distant past. This is part of the effect of the disease on the brain. They also recall the "feeling" of a conversation even if they do not remember the actual words. This makes it even more important to keep the topic neutral when conversing. If an argument or some kind of negative conversation transpires, the elder may forget what was said but "remember" that the conversation was unpleasant, therefore, making it difficult to shift the behavior in a positive direction. They will also react to tone of voice, facial expressions, and word choices and may respond negatively simply because they find the communication confusing.

Practicing Good Hygiene

Getting a good history of the elder's previous habits and self-care practices is important. Knowing the details of their daily personal and oral care, including preferred brands of toothpaste, bath soap, shampoo, and so forth, can make these tasks easier to manage. Does their body temperature run cold or hot? In the past, did they prefer to use a shower or a tub? How do they feel about being touched? What are their toileting habits? The more a companion knows about the elder's preferences, the easier (and smoother) it will be to practice good hygiene.

NOTES

Showering/bathing and healthy hygiene processes can be among the most challenging activities for a companion caring for a person with dementia. Even older adults without dementia can get to a point where they resist bathing, feeling as though it's too much effort or a bit of a battle. As mentioned above, daily bathing may not be necessary, as older adults do not sweat very much. Every other day or as little as twice a week can suffice with many elders with just some freshening up on the days in between. The elder can use disposable wipes on days when they don't take a shower or wash with a washcloth under the armpits and in the genital area. Larger wipes are available, including unscented brands if the elder's skin is fragrance sensitive.

In the early to middle stages of dementia, it may not be as difficult to get the elder to take a bath or shower, but as the disease progresses, bathing can become more of a challenge. At any time, the elder may feel like their privacy is being invaded, which can lead to resistance. Companions should allow the elder to do most or all the tasks on their own, though they must "stand by" to make sure they can come to the rescue if needed. "Stand by" in the early stages of the disease may mean just being within earshot of the bathroom, so you can hear if the elder needs assistance. Also, as the disease progresses through the middle stage, the elder may require more instructions but still not need the companion to physically touch them.

Some elders in the earlier stages of the disease may be fine taking a bath rather than a shower, though bathing can present challenges not only for the elder to get out of the tub (for weaker adults), but the process of taking a bath can be a bit more complex as well. For instance, getting the temperature just right and keeping it at the perfect warmth throughout the bath can be difficult, especially if the elder likes to soak or refuses help. Still, if taking a bath is the elder's preference and there are no safety issues, then a bath is perfectly fine.

The goal is to make the task of bathing or showering as positive of an experience as possible. Encouraging expressions like, "It's time for your bath now," or if there's push back you might say, "You always feel so good after your bath/shower." In some cases, it may be possible for a companion to take a shower ahead of the elder and then comment on how wonderful they feel as they are toweling off.

In most cases, it's best to give the shower during the same general time of day that the elder has historically bathed. Be sure to have everything prepared ahead of time and placed where the elder is used to finding them, such as soap, shampoo, washcloths, and towels. The companion could even add liquid soap to the washcloth and then hand it to the elder. The room should be warm, so consider using a small space heater. Have the elder's favorite robe hanging where they can see it, so they know they will be able to cover themself when they come out of the shower or bathtub. The companion can place a clean, dry towel on a chair or bench in the bathroom if space allows, so the elder can sit down when they get out of the shower or tub. Be gentle and respectful, calmly explaining what needs to be done, step by step.

The best-equipped shower or bathtub should have plenty of handrails with a long rail on each side wall and at least one vertical rail for exiting the shower. A hand-held shower head is best for showering assistance from outside the shower. The companion can get the shower ready by removing the shower head from the holder while setting the water temperature as desired, then placing the shower head back in the holder, turned to face the wall, so no one gets wet. The elder then turns the shower head downward, toward them, once they are in. It's also a good practice to have the elder feel the water temperature before hanging the showerhead up, so they can maintain a sense of control about what they are stepping into. The elder can be instructed to first test the temperature with their hands or feet.

Of course, there should be a rubber mat to prevent slipping, and if the elder prefers to sit, a sturdy shower chair. Soft music can be a nice addition to keep the experience calm and inviting. One helpful item is a shower curtain that is see-through in the upper portion. The elder and companion can see one another for ease of communication, and the companion can discreetly watch to ensure the elder is cleaning all parts of their body. (See the link to a sample shower curtain on the Resources page on our website.)

When the showering is complete, the companion can hand a towel to the elder while they are still in the shower with the curtain closed to keep the warm air in, allowing them to dry themself off in comfort and privacy. A number of towel warmers are available to purchase and can be a great selling point for the elder when trying to convince them to shower. The companion can even heat the elder's robe ahead of time. (This is a real luxury for anyone, but especially for elders, as they often feel quite chilled after bathing.) Feeling cold is often a deterrent to bathing, so keeping the air in the bathroom warm and having warm towels can be helpful.

Older skin can be fragile, so if the elder is too rough with their drying technique, gently suggest they go easier and dab or pat themself dry instead of rubbing. They may only dry themself partially, and that's fine. They can wrap the towel around their body and come out of the shower. Using a second towel, the companion can pat dry the wet areas to finish the job. This can be partially done while the elder is standing on the bath rug and finished when they sit down. If there's no room in the bathroom for a chair, the elder could sit on the toilet. Be sure to get the elder's feet dry between the toes as well as body crevices, either by instructing or helping them do so.

Keeping an elder's skin well hydrated and healthy is important. If the elder has sensitivities to fragrances, be sure to purchase lotions or oils appropriate for their needs. They can apply lotion to dry areas daily or a few times a week, such as after bathing. Each morning or evening it's a good habit to have them wash their face and apply a good moisturizing lotion before or after brushing their teeth. Other areas of dry skin can be addressed at the same time. Take into consideration that less frequent showers may help with dry skin issues.

Also, a good routine to create is having the individual wash their hands in the morning after they get up, whether they use the toilet or not. This is essential if they use the commode during the night. Making sure the water from the faucet is a pleasing temperature makes this small but important hygiene task more inviting.

In the later stages of dementia, the elder may require more hands-on help while showering. YouTube has some good videos on how to bathe a person with dementia who is refusing to cooperate. Some videos even show how to bathe a person in their bed without getting them soaking wet. Try searching phrases like, "videos for bathing persons with dementia," and "complete bed bath." At this stage, the family can look into having a professional come in once a week to help with bathing if it becomes too challenging for the companions (or if the 20 percent of caregiving is close to being exceeded). Showering once a week may be sufficient as long as companions can give sponge baths in between showers, for example, by utilizing disposable wipes or cloths after an incontinence incident.

A significant part of keeping the elder clean is making sure they are wiping correctly after using the bathroom. Women need to wipe from front to back to avoid contaminating the urethra, which can cause urinary tract infections. A bidet that is attached to the toilet is an effective tool to help with hygiene if getting clean after toileting is an issue.

Practicing Oral Hygiene

Good oral hygiene is extremely important. Experiencing a dental visit for an elder with dementia who needs a filling, for example, is enough for a companion to become diligent with dental care. If possible, the companion can brush their own teeth while standing next to the elder every morning and night as a routine activity of daily living (ADL). This task may require brushing one's teeth at the kitchen sink unless the bathroom has two sinks. Brushing one's teeth is typically an engrained daily habit for most and likely won't require a lot of prompts until the later stages of dementia. Electric toothbrushes and three-sided toothbrushes are helpful for people with dementia. (See the link to a sample toothbrush on the Resources page on our website.)

Habitual behaviors, such as brushing one's teeth and getting dressed, are well-implanted in the brain, and it's likely the elder can continue doing these things for quite some time. It's more likely, however, that the individual simply won't want to brush their teeth, so standing right next to them can usually be enough encouragement. In the later stages, Lucy sometimes would watch the companion for clues on how to do simple hygiene-related tasks. This was evident when she brushed her hair with her toothbrush and got toothpaste in her hair. Demonstrating tasks became more necessary as the disease advanced.

After brushing, have the elder floss their teeth while you floss yours or use a handheld flossing pick. If the elder is able to use a Waterpik, most dentists encourage this; just be sure to set the water temperature as desired beforehand. Having the elder use the Waterpik in the shower is another method that may work well, as controlling the water spray can be an issue once they are dressed and dry.

Incontinence

As the disease of dementia progresses, incontinence becomes more common. There's no sugar coating it: dealing with incontinence is an unpleasant task. Handling incontinence can be extremely uncomfortable for both parties and often embarrassing for the elder. At this point, scheduling bathroom breaks every two hours can be helpful. Using a phone app or kitchen timer helps prevent accidents from occurring, as well as simply asking the individual periodically if they need to use the toilet.

Putting a portable commode in the bedroom for nighttime use is helpful. If possible, position it by an outlet, so you can plug in a nightlight behind or beneath the commode to enhance visibility from the individual's bed. Put approximately two inches of clean water in the commode to avoid splashing during urination, to subdue odor from bowel movements, and to offer greater ease while emptying the contents into a toilet.

The elder should wear an absorbent undergarment at all times during the advanced stage of dementia, and the bed must have a waterproof pad as opposed to a water-repellent pad. Furthermore, we suggest augmenting the mattress protection

NOTES

with washable, moisture-absorbent cloth pads on top of the fitted sheet. The companion can put these into the wash easily without having to change all the sheets. These pads are also handy to use on couches and chairs or in the car, but they may require being pinned to stay in place.

A couple of other handy items are a diaper hamper for soiled disposable undergarments and an airtight trash can with removable liners for wet pads and clothing; both items help keep odors in check. (See samples on the Resources page on our website.)

In some circumstances, incontinence is not regular enough to justify having the elder wear a bulky undergarment at all times, especially during the daytime. However, when on outings, it's wise to either have the elder wear a protective undergarment or take an "emergency kit" along. The kit can be in the form of a cloth or paper bag, consisting of a spare pair of underwear, pants, disposable wipes, vinyl gloves, and a plastic bag to put soiled garments in. To save the elder from an embarrassing situation, it might be best to have them put on the undergarment before going out or ask often while on the outing if they need to use the bathroom.

An article on www.AgingCare.com, titled "UTIs and Dementia in Seniors: Impact and Treatment Options," stresses that since incontinence can be caused by urinary tract infections (UTIs), a sudden onset of incontinence should be reported right away to the elder's family or care manager. A little-known fact is that, in elders, urinary tract infections often manifest differently, with an increase in confusion, agitation, and delirium that comes on quite suddenly, sometimes without the pain that is commonly experienced with these types of infections.

According to an article published on www.WebMD.com, titled "When a UTI Gets Complicated," a UTI that is not treated right away can, in rare cases, become life threatening. Medically treating a UTI can sometimes solve the problem of incontinence, at least in the short run. However, since dementia patients are more prone to getting UTIs, they may reoccur, especially during the later stages of the disease.

Though it may seem counterproductive, making sure the elder drinks plenty of water or other liquids throughout the day is probably one of the best preventive measures against UTIs. Dehydration is common in people with dementia, largely because they forget to drink or think that they're hungry when they are actually thirsty and need hydration. Dehydration can lead to a UTI and can contribute to constipation, which also causes great discomfort to the elder.

One way to avoid dehydration is to find quality drinks that the elder enjoys. Ideally, these should be noncarbonated, low in sugar or sugar free, and caffeine free. A few suggestions are decaffeinated or herbal teas served hot or iced, naturally flavored waters, and unsweetened or watered-down cranberry juice. Note: Mixed fruit juices are tasty but also contain a substantial amount of sugar. Coconut water is another excellent choice, as it has naturally occurring electrolytes, such as potassium, sodium, and manganese.

The "UTIs and Dementia in Seniors" article on www.AgingCare.com stresses that the necessary amount of fluid intake varies per the individual and should be dictated by one's physician. For some medical conditions, too much liquid can be detrimental. In general, it is a good idea to avoid liquids just before bedtime, making it essential to drink enough fluids during the day.

Managing Sundowning

Sundowning is when an elder experiences an increase in confusion, anxiety, agitation, pacing, and disorientation beginning in the late afternoon and often continuing well into the night. There can be triggers to sundowning, and learning what those are in the person being cared for can help manage the behavior. This subject is covered in more detail in Chapter 10: Common Behaviors of People with Dementia.

Here are some ideas to help the companion shift behaviors associated with sundowning:

- Reduce nighttime stimulation.

- Have the largest meal at lunch with a lighter dinner.

- Keep the home well-lit in the late afternoon and evening.

- Find soothing activities to do in the evenings, such as listening to calming music or watching calming videos.

- Have the family or care manager check with the doctor about the best times of day for taking medications.

- Ensure the elder avoids alcohol, caffeine, and nicotine too late in the day.

- Take a walk to help reduce restlessness; this can even be around the inside of the house.

- Companions should make sure they are not exhibiting stress or unintended nonverbal distress.

Every person with dementia is different, so finding what works for any given individual may take some time and effort. In the long run, finding what works is worthwhile, because sundowning can affect the length and quality of sleep a companion is able to get, which directly impacts how well they can care for the elder during the day. If the person with dementia suffers from sundowning, the companions may have to stick with only working a two-day shift, because three days without good sleep may be too difficult.

Making and Keeping Schedules for the Elder

An article on www.AgingCare.com, titled "The Importance of Creating a Daily Routine for Dementia Patients," addresses the importance of routines and schedules for a person with dementia, particularly during the middle to late stages of the disease. With Lucy, we observed that she best retained the memory of how to do activities when she continued to do them on a regular basis. She was fluent in American Sign Language and could call it up easily, so the companions would encourage her to sign for them.

Dressing and self-care activities came naturally to Lucy, as they do for most people, but with dementia, over time even those simple acts become more of a challenge. Having a somewhat consistent schedule can help implant the familiar and be settling for someone with dementia. A regular schedule helps the companions as well, because they don't have to constantly come up with activities to do during the day.

Before making a planned schedule, it's good to take into consideration a few factors. The Alzheimer's Association suggests considering the following:

- The elder's likes, dislikes, strengths, abilities, and interests

- The structure of the elder's day in the past or perhaps most of their life

- The time of day the elder functions best and using that time for more challenging activities

- Regular times to go to bed and get up in the morning (especially helpful if the elder has sleep or sundowning issues)

The Sample Daily Routine Schedule (Figure 2) represents what a daily schedule could look like. This is not to say that everything on the list takes the amount of time allocated; the sample represents periods of time within which a companion and an elder might do certain activities. The daily routine should be somewhat flexible to allow for spontaneous activities as well.

NOTES

Sample Daily Routine Schedule		
8:00 a.m.	8:30 a.m.	Rise and get dressed.
8:30 a.m.	9:00 a.m.	Have quiet time while the companion makes breakfast (for example, a simple meditation, video, music, or sitting quietly).
9:00 a.m.	9:30 a.m.	Eat breakfast together.
9:30 a.m.	10:00 a.m.	Have personal care time (brush teeth, wash face, or take a shower).
10:00 a.m.	12:00 p.m.	Enjoy free-time activities around the house (music, crafts, hobbies, reading, and so forth).
12:00 p.m.	12:30 p.m.	Make lunch together or open time for elder while companion makes lunch.
12:30 p.m.	1:00 p.m.	Eat lunch together.
1:00 p.m.	4:00 p.m.	Go on a spontaneous outing, for a walk, or visit a friend.
4:00 p.m.	5:00 p.m.	Do household chores (fold laundry, put dishes away, make the bed, and so forth).
5:00 p.m.	6:00 p.m.	Exercise such as PT, OT, chair yoga, qigong, easy stretching (usually guided on TV) while companion makes dinner, or the elder can help in the kitchen as they are able and willing.
6:00 p.m.	7:00 p.m.	Eat dinner together.
7:00 p.m.	9:30 p.m.	Open time for entertainment (watching TV, reading, playing a game, and so forth).
9:30 p.m.	10:00 p.m.	Bedtime routine (use toilet, brush teeth, put on pajamas, read in bed).

Figure 2. Sample Daily Routine Schedule

There will likely come a time when incontinence becomes an issue; thus, setting an alarm for a scheduled bathroom break every two hours can help avoid accidents. The morning, noon, and bedtime routines are the most important, partly because the elder may need to take medications and, partly, to have a set schedule that allows the companion and elder to get a full night's sleep.

You can use a whiteboard to record a daily schedule, so the elder knows what lies ahead for the day. This could include fun projects, chores, appointments, and outings to the park or local coffee shop.

Companions' Work Schedules and Shift Crossovers

One of the more appealing aspects of the Purple Nest Home Care Model is the flexibility allowed for scheduling the work week for the companions. Our model suggests three full-time companions and one backup companion. Typically, each of the three full-time people works a 48-hour shift four to five times per month, and the backup person works one to three days per month or is simply on call and does not necessarily work every month. (Scheduling is discussed in more detail in Chapter 3: Phases of Care; additionally, you can find sample schedules on the Printable Documents page on our website, www.ThePurpleNest.net.)

In Lucy's case, we typically followed the model exactly as explained above. One of the four team members was a retired nurse who had the flexibility to work on an as-needed basis. Another backup companion owned her own business and wanted to augment her income, so again, she had flexibility.

During the summer months and holiday season, the backup companions could expect more shifts due to vacation requests made by the three core companions. Each month the companions would communicate which days they wanted off, and then everyone worked out the schedule mid-month for the following month. It often worked out that a companion could have six to ten days off in a row during the month and still work eight, nine, or ten days during the month. This scheduling method meant that the care team did not have set days that they always worked. However, in months where no one requested a special stretch of days off in a row, the schedule would usually work out to consistently be two days on followed by four days off, logically falling on different days as the weeks progressed.

Lucy's companions experimented with various scheduling approaches. One scheduling option that worked quite well for the three companions was to work set days every week (in two-day shifts) with the seventh day being open for either a companion to work a three-day shift or for the backup person to come in that seventh day. In this scheduling option, every core companion is assured, at the very least, eight days of work (four two-day shifts) per month. This set schedule frees up companions to take on other work if they choose. In Lucy's case, several companions spent time with another client for a few hours or an entire day, one or two times a week.

As we developed the Purple Nest Home Care Model, we tested several different shift start/end times. (Remember that in this care model the companions' shifts are 24 hours, 48 hours, or 72 hours.) The shift start/end times included 9:00 a.m., 11:00 a.m., 12:00 p.m., 7:30 p.m., and, finally, 7:00 p.m. We discovered that the ideal shift start/end time depends largely on the routine of the elder. For instance, 9:00 a.m.

NOTES

NOTES

and 11:00 a.m. were too early for Lucy, because the morning routines (primarily breakfast and bathing) could not be completed by those times, so it was better to finish breakfast and showering before the next companion arrived.

Arriving at 12:00 p.m. (noon) required the companion coming on duty to immediately start preparing lunch. For the companion leaving at 12:00 p.m. it was a challenge to complete the end-of-shift household chores. That said, the 12:00 p.m. shift start/end time did work well overall and was used for many months.

Finally, the companions determined that the 7:00 p.m. shift change worked best for this care team and Lucy. When starting at this time, dinner was already finished, and the beginning of the shift was easy to adjust to for both the elder and the companion. Basically, the newly arriving companion came in to spend the evening in a leisurely way with only about three hours until bedtime. This schedule allowed the companion who was leaving to make plans on the evening after their shift ended. Of course, if the elder is a nighttime bather, the companion coming in may have to take care of that task, but the bulk of the "real work" takes place in the next two days (before the shift ended at 7:00 p.m. 48 hours later). Also, if the elder experiences severe sundowning, then a shift change in the evening might not be ideal. The ideal shift-change time depends on the needs of the elder and the care team.

We suggest that the companion arrives ten to fifteen minutes early to allow for shift crossover conversations and to allow the elder to adjust to the arrival of the next companion. Depending on what's going on with the elder, it can take as long as thirty minutes to do a thorough crossover, so for fairness, we recommend that each companion "gives" fifteen minutes. In other words, one companion arrives fifteen minutes before the shift change, and one departs fifteen minutes after the shift ends. Of course, much of what needs to be relayed is in the daily notes, so if nothing out of the ordinary is going on, for example, treatment for an illness or demonstrating physical therapy exercises, the crossover can take as little as ten minutes. Often, the companions just want to hang out awhile and visit, which the elder enjoys as well.

As the companions refined the Purple Nest Home Care Model with Lucy's care, shift changes were generally less stressful for Lucy, but another elder might feel anxious and benefit from a short gathering in the living room where it feels more like company has stopped by for a visit. It can be a little awkward, especially when the companions need to discuss something confidentially. If the elder is content watching TV while the companions converse, that's fine too. Creating a situation in which someone feels like they're being talked about as though they're invisible isn't pleasant for anyone, so it's important for the companions to find ways to communicate that work best for everyone.

Communication and Reporting

Companions must record the day's events—we cannot stress this enough. Whether the companions handwrite their notes on printed pages in a binder or record their notes online in a Google doc, the data recorded in these notes are important. You may want to consider workplace communication tools (such as Asana) and apps that include video (such as Slack, Marco Polo, and WhatsApp) to capture and simplify information gathering. The companions of an elder with dementia are their number-one observers and, therefore, their best advocates.

The daily entries report any health concerns to the care manager or family member in charge of the elder's health, and they also help the whole team of companions stay on top of how the elder is doing in general. The notes also contain helpful information the care manager or family can pass on to the medical care team as necessary. (See the Daily Progress Notes template on the Printable Documents page on our website.)

The daily progress notes should record what the companion and elder did during their time together and include how much the elder enjoyed the activities, or not. The companion should also report changes in the elder's behavior or anything that's concerning. For example, the elder has a new sore that needs to be tended to or is healing nicely. This is the place to report hallucinations, illusions, sundowning, and so forth, and it's also the place to relay joyful times, like a funny story that may have happened during the day. If the companion and elder made cookies together, write which parts of the activity the elder did or wasn't comfortable doing. Companions could also record what the individual ate at each meal, the elder's weight, bowel movements, and hygiene tasks.

The family or care manager decides the type of information they want to see on the daily progress notes. The entries in the daily log do not have to list every single thing done during the day; they are more about recording activities that went really great, as well as situations that went sideways or were upsetting to the elder. Companions should record and share their notes either daily or at the end of the shift (whatever the family has decided) with whoever has been designated to receive them.

The companions may also want to have a journal for just their team, which would include helpful notes that pertain to running the home and do not necessarily need to be given to the care manager or family. The Companions' Journal may include details about gardening, unplugging a sink, purchases of special items for the home, a more efficient cleaning method, updates on a decluttering project, and so forth. While there is a crossover at each shift change, the companions may not have time to discuss details outside of those relayed about the elder's care; thus, knowing that the team journal exists to read about the home at a later time is invaluable!

Another helpful tool is having a large whiteboard and markers to record a daily schedule, so the elder knows what lies ahead for the day. This could include fun projects, chores, appointments, and outings to the park or local coffee shop. In addition, a whiteboard is a helpful tool for recording current treatments or regimens. For example, sometimes the elder may need pain medications, such as Tylenol and ibuprofen, and it's important to note the times of the day and dosages of the medications given. This can be particularly useful after surgery or during recovery from an illness. The companions can use the whiteboard to keep track of treatments outside of any regular medication regimens.

It is important to research medication administration in the state in which the elder lives, as the care team must follow all state-specific rules. For instance, "reminding" might be distinguished from "administering"; the latter may require a skilled or licensed individual, such as an RN. Various medication management tools can help everyone remain compliant with state medication administration rules. For example, specialized pharmacies will bubble pack all daily medications, so all the medications are in one bubble per day (or two or three depending on how many times an elder takes their medications during the day). All the elder needs to do is pop the bubble and take their meds. Additionally, medication dispensers are helpful for dispensing daily medications. A family member or nurse can fill it monthly and thus eliminate the need for the companions to be involved in medication disbursement. Finally, the family can fill med boxes on a bimonthly or monthly basis, and the companions can simply remind the elder to open the appropriate box and take their meds.

Housecleaning and Being a Team Player

At the end of a shift, it's important to leave the home in good shape for the next companion. While companions need to do light housekeeping chores on most days, such as laundry and dishes, they also need to address a short list of basic upkeep items that should be checked off at the end of each companion's shift. As a reminder, the housekeeping chores are part of the caregiving responsibilities, and those must be kept to 20 percent of activities over the course of a shift (one, two, or three days). The short checklist consists mostly of good habits and respecting the next person coming in, and often, the tasks have already been taken care of throughout the day. (See the template End-of-Shift Checklist on the Printable Documents page on our website.)

An end-of-shift checklist usually includes such items as:

1. Kitchen counters are clear and clean, and a fresh hand towel has been hung.

2. Dishwasher has been run—unless half full or less—and clean dishes put away.

3. Kitchen floor has been swept.

4. Trash and recycle items have been taken out when the trash can and recycle bin are full.

5. Laundry has been done with no more than half a hamper left to wash.

6. All bathrooms are clean and tidy, and fresh hand towels have been hung.

7. The companions' bed has been stripped, so the next companion can make the bed with their sheets.

8. Living areas are generally tidied up.

9. Note: If there are pets in the home, the vacuum may need to be run more frequently.

Changes in the elder's needs can make it more difficult to check off every item on the list all the time. Sometimes laundry may need to be folded and put away, or perhaps the dishwasher isn't finished running, but, in general, the companions should do their best to take care of these items before their shift ends. The home should be in basically the same condition when the companion leaves as it was when they arrived.

Another good practice is for the companions to take turns cleaning out the refrigerator, freezer, and pantry at least once a month, though, of course, it's important to keep on top of spoiling food on a daily basis. In addition, the companions should make sure the elder's sheets are washed on a regular basis, as decided by the family or care manager. All these items can be put on a Google calendar (or a calendar of choice) along with changing furnace filters or water purification filters, washing bathroom rugs and curtains, or any other periodic maintenance chores. (See the General Home Management Task List on the Printable Documents page on our website.)

Many of these chores do not take more than a few minutes, and companions should always involve the elder whenever possible. It makes them feel useful and involved, and they may even find the chores fun! Lucy loved to help the companions make and unmake their beds, which is one chore that is "friendlier with two." Other chores, such as putting dishes away and folding laundry, are great ways to keep the elder busy and using their brain and hands, particularly putting silverware in the compartments of the silverware drawer. It's OK if including the elder means getting things done takes a little longer; part of the purpose of these activities is to keep the elder active, which falls under companionship.

While keeping the home neat and tidy is important from a safety standpoint, making it spotless is not in the job description. The family will likely hire a company to come in at least once a month to do a thorough cleaning, or if a companion would like additional hourly work, that's a possibility as well. When everyone does their part, home upkeep is easier and has less chance of becoming a source of contention as "clean" can mean different things to different people. That said, the day-to-day overarching duty of a companion is to spend quality time with the elder, doing the things they enjoy, while keeping them focused and as active as possible.

Fulfillment and Rewards

Working as a companion for a person with dementia can be a rewarding experience for a number of reasons. When keeping in mind that the job of a companion is to make the elder's last days as joyful as possible, it sets the tone for the whole experience. The companions who worked with Lucy treated her with the utmost respect and spoke to her as a friend. This fostered a lot of cooperation, particularly during the middle stages of dementia, and both parties enjoyed the days equally. There was little time for boredom, though they carried out activities at a sometimes slower pace set by Lucy.

It might be helpful to think of the mind of the person with dementia as operating in a simpler capacity. In doing so, the companion can also be reminded of the simpler things in life that make us all happy, such as enjoying the changing of the seasons in all their specific grandeur or watching children play on the playground. Also, socializing with folks while walking in the neighborhood or "people watching" in a park can be rewarding. Going for an ice cream or a picnic may be activities we associate more with our childhoods, but we don't stop enjoying them; usually we just stop doing them.

When we can encourage and bring out the best in a person with dementia, we may be rewarded in ways we would have never expected. One case in point is the story about Lucy using sign language while she sang along with hymns on YouTube. Those ingrained learned activities that she had done so much of her life were inside of her. Once the companions got a glimpse of those behaviors, they were able to encourage her to do them again, to the joy of everyone. Sometimes Lucy would show her gratitude by saying, "Thank you for doing all of this," accompanied by a kiss on the cheek or forehead. Talk about heart melting! Finding activities that bring the elder joy and repeating them helps tremendously with their mood, which, in turn, helps the companion's mood.

As mentioned in the section above, "How to Talk to a Person with Dementia," the companion can set the tone of communication. Is it tedious to keep repeating the same answers over and over throughout the day? Yes. Can the companion choose to distract the elder instead of getting frustrated? Yes. Will that always work? No. Some behaviors will drive the companion up a wall. That reality supports the reasoning for keeping shifts to 48 hours, particularly as the elder moves into the later stages of the disease. Some companions have a greater capacity to deal with dementia behaviors and may be fine with longer shifts, and that is great when this is the case. However, it is essential to avoid caregiver burnout, which is a common occurrence for companions of dementia clients, although far less likely in the Purple Nest Home Care Model, because there are longer breaks in between shifts.

It is said that with dementia there are two patients: the elder and their caregiver, especially if there is only one main caregiver. The companion/caregiver in this model needs to practice good self-care as well, especially when the disease progresses and this person, who has become a friend, begins to fade toward their setting sun. The companion should always make time for themselves each day they are working. Find the best time to take a shower, perhaps before the elder awakes or after they go to bed. As much as possible, get good sleep, and don't let anything you are doing for your health (such as taking vitamins or medications) slip through the cracks. While it is certainly easier physically to be part of a team, rather than a lone caregiver, psychologically and emotionally there are still challenging times.

From the start, patience is a prerequisite for this job. If a person has patience, along with a good dose of compassion and a strong desire to help people, being a companion can be fulfilling work. The rewards can far outweigh the challenges!

A Note about Boundaries

Yes, being a companion can be rewarding, but it is also hard work, and it can be taxing and even frustrating at times. For this reason, practicing good boundaries is important. While we talk about treating the elder as a friend or equal, it is also important to remember that the companion is working in a professional capacity and should act like a professional. Part of having good boundaries and acting professionally is knowing and protecting your personal limits and respecting the boundaries of the elder and all members of the care team. This includes maintaining confidentiality about the elder's health condition, finances, and all personal information concerning the elder and their family.

The companion should not accept gifts, whether material or financial, from the elder unless they have been expressly approved by the party responsible for the elder's finances, whether that is the family, care manager, or daily money manager. Likewise, the companion should not consume or use alcohol, marijuana, or other substances (that could alter the companion's ability to think clearly) while on duty, even if the elder does. Anything can happen at any hour of the day or night, and the companion must be ready and able to respond to unforeseen situations at all times. Because these matters are of utmost importance, the companions' employment contract should include verbiage surrounding these topics.

Companion Checklist

The following onboarding checklist for a newly hired companion will help the team track essential paperwork and help the companion learn the essentials of the position. The newly hired companion should complete items one through four as quickly as possible. They should complete the remaining tasks within the first two to four weeks of employment. The companion should initial each numbered item when completed and turn in the paperwork to the person who hired them. (You can download this checklist from our website on the Printable Documents page.)

We suggest dating each item as it is completed.

Complete and provide all onboarding documents listed below and turn them in to the hiring agent:		
1		Sign Form I-9 (Employment Eligibility Verification Form from the Department of Homeland Security).
2		Provide proof of current car insurance (if applicable).
3		Provide proof of valid driver's license—photocopy of both front and back.
4		Provide a copy of your driving record from the department of motor vehicles in your state; ask the hiring agent if reimbursement of expense is a possibility.
5		Provide proof of completed background check; ask the hiring agent if reimbursement of expense is a possibility.
6		Complete all payroll-related paperwork (for example, Form W-4, direct-deposit forms, possible voided check of bank account).
7		Notify hiring agent of any pending garnishments you might have.
8		Sign Companion Contract (if applicable, with each page initialed).
9		Provide the best phone number and email address for the home care team to use for you.
10		Notify the hiring agent if your legal name is different from the name you are using with the team.

11		Read the Home Care Companion Handbook and Addendum thoroughly and refer any questions to the hiring agent.
12		Become familiar with the process of completing the regular payroll paperwork (including completing a timesheet, learning how to sign in to the payroll company employee account portal, if applicable, and so forth).
13		Become familiar with the shared online calendar and establish access on your phone or personal computer. This is a critical tool, as it contains all important appointments as well as the work schedule.

Become familiar with the elder's home.

(All this will be shown during the training sessions; however, it may be a lot of information all at once and easy to forget the details. This list can help those who conduct the training as well as those receiving the training.)

You will basically be running the house while you are there, so you must know where everything is kept including:

14		Bed and bath supplies (for both the elder and yourself)
15		Elder's clothes and grooming supplies
16		Elder's personal care items, such as hearing aids, eyeglasses, dentures, and glucose monitors
17		House-cleaning supplies (including vacuum, brooms/ Swiffers, snow shovel, and so forth)
18		Washer, dryer, and laundry supplies
19		Food storage (cupboards and pantries)
20		Paper products, such as paper towels and toilet paper
21		House keys (including the location of any spare or hidden keys)
22		Arts and crafts supplies
23		How to work TV remotes and any other remotes
24		How to log on to laptops, other computers, tablets
25		How to log on to WIFI
26		How to work baby monitors or child gates

27		How to access voicemail on the home phone and cell phone
28		How to activate and deactivate all alarm systems, including garage entry (if applicable)
Become familiar with the elder's medical team—particularly the phone numbers and addresses, as you will be transporting the elder to appointments. *(This information is in the Addendum of the Home Care Companion Handbook.)*		
29		Become familiar with medications and supplements: how and when they are administered, where they are kept, how they are ordered, whether the elder requires instructions, or if the elder is cooperative with taking medications. Be sure to clarify whether the elder has any allergies.
30		Know which hospital is the primary one for the elder's insurance for non-life-threatening emergencies and which one is nearest the home (this information is in the Addendum).
31		Know where the Emergency Packet is kept in case of an emergency, as outlined in the Home Care Companion Handbook.
32		Be aware of any rules established by the family, care manager, or medical team concerning the care of the elder, including dietary stipulations. (Again, this information is in the Home Care Companion Handbook.)
33		Know where to find the elder's insurance cards, debit or credit cards, checkbooks, and IDs to be used as directed by the employer. All applicable items should be in a small purse that is carried when taking the elder on an outing.
34		Become familiar with the idiosyncrasies of the elder. This will happen over time, but be sure you know up front about any triggers that can produce unwanted behaviors. On the flip side, also familiarize yourself with any actions you can take to get the elder out of that behavior. (These details are in the Home Care Companion Handbook.)
35		Become familiar with filling out daily notes (whether in a binder or online). These are submitted at the end of every shift to the family or care manager.

NOTES

NOTES

36		Become familiar with the places the elder likes to go to on outings, how long it takes to get there, the schedules surrounding these activities, and whether they require payment (for example, yoga classes, aerobic swimming, tai chi, etc.).
37		Become familiar with meal planning and grocery shopping (for example, the elder's favorite foods, where the household generally shops, and how to minimize trips by communicating with other companions and picking up items for them).
38		If you are reimbursed by the elder for your mileage, purchase a mileage tracker or keep a notebook and pen in your car for those times when you take the elder in your car to an appointment or outing. You will need this information when completing your mileage reimbursement form.
39		Become familiar with the End-of-Shift Checklist, which should be posted in a common area. This list includes items that take only a few minutes each day but help to keep the home in a tidy state. This checklist helps ensure consistency and fairness among the companions.
40		Become familiar with the Companions' Journal if applicable. This is for communication concerning running the home and used only by the companions themselves. It is not essential but can be a helpful tool.
41		Become familiar with pet care if applicable. (Veterinarian information and dietary needs are in the Addendum of the Home Care Companion Handbook.)

CHAPTER 7
Branch Four: The Care Manager

This chapter explores the many helpful tasks a care manager (CM) can take on when caring for an elder with dementia, as well as anyone who might benefit from having someone help manage their care. The care manager is there to help the individual and their family navigate through the changes and needs as they arise due to the progression of the disease.

The care manager effectively takes over communicating with the elder's entire medical team. This can include general practitioners, neurologists, dentists, optometrists, naturopathic doctors, chiropractors, and any other health care professional treating the elder. The CM can also accompany the elder to all important medical-related appointments and is in charge of keeping medical notes and records, including tracking medications. The CM takes on the responsibility of updating the home care team—which includes the family or whoever has been designated as the medical power of attorney or health care representative, companions, and daily money manager (if applicable)—on the current medical status as well as any changes concerning the health care of the elder.

The care manager may also coach the family on the process of hiring the companions and managing them, including scheduling, training, and supervision. In some states the care manager may not be able to directly hire, train, or schedule the companions without being a registered care agency. In these states, assuming the care manager prefers not to register as a care agency, the CM can only coach or advise the family on these companion-related tasks. The family or care manager should research this with the state's Health Authority. If the CM is authorized to take on the management of the companions, it can be a huge help to the family. The care management duties are already an enormous load off the family's plate, and other responsibilities spelled out in this chapter can be turned over to the CM as well.

One of the most important tasks the care manager performs is monitoring for abuse and reporting known or suspected abuse. Elders with dementia are particularly vulnerable to all types of abuse: financial, physical, sexual, emotional, and neglect. Since people with dementia often have a difficult time expressing themselves and may forget instances of abuse, the care manager needs to be vigilant of this possibility and look for signs that might suggest mistreatment is occurring, such as suspicious injuries or bruises, fearful or withdrawn behavior, increased behavioral issues, dirty clothing, body odor, or skin rashes and breakdown in the genital area. Financial abuse is the most common form of elder abuse; if the family has hired a daily money manager, this person is in a position to monitor for any misuse of funds that might occur. Mandated reporting laws are different depending on the state. In some states anyone who is in the position of caring for elders is mandated by law to report abuse or suspected abuse to the authorities (often referred to as Adult Protective Services). Social workers and medical professionals are trained to identify abuse and are mandated in all states to report abuse.

Finding a Care Manager

If the family decides to hire a professional care manager, you can search for a CM in a number of places. Geriatric care managers specialize in working with the elderly, but the role can be filled by social workers, nurses, psychologists, or by gerontologists who specialize in elder care management. A family member, a friend, or even one of the companions can perform the duties of the CM. That said, the role can be quite time consuming, as it requires impeccable record keeping, so hiring a professional CM can be advantageous. Also, if a companion takes on the role, they must perform the duties of the care manager outside of the hours they work directly with the elder in order to maintain the FLSA 80/20 rule discussed in Chapter 3: Phases of Care. No matter who takes on the duties of a care manager, if that person quits or leaves for any reason, the family should request their records.

You can search for a care manager in any state at www.AgingLifeCare.org, a nationwide professional organization that credentials geriatric care managers. It is not required, however, to be credentialed, and you can also find care managers on www.Caring.com or by doing a Google search in your area. Elder law attorneys are also an excellent resource for finding local care managers.

Tasks Performed by a Care Manager

The tasks required and the amount of time each will take vary based on the situation, the stage of the disease, and the organization of the home. Some situations are fairly cut and dry; others are more complicated. For instance, if an elder has lived in their home for decades, there could be a significant need to do some clutter clearing. The CM does not usually get involved with the tasks of clearing the home but will identify the safety issues surrounding the state of the elder's home. They may advise on how or where to get help with decluttering, especially if they have worked with a professional organizer in the past.

The first task that the CM usually completes is an assessment, which generally takes place over one or two visits and includes an interview with the elder, a tour of the residence, a review of the medical records, and a conversation with family and friends who might have the social and medical history of the elder.

During the assessment process the CM should interview the family and the elder on a history of trauma including past sexual or physical abuse. These histories can become especially important when providing personal care to a dementia patient. In this same vein it is also important to ask about a history of self-harming behaviors or aggression toward others. These behaviors can reemerge with dementia. The assessment can include a written document with recommendations and a care plan if requested.

It is helpful to enlist the help of a home health agency in the assessment process. With a release of information (ROI) form, the CM can ask the elder's doctor for a referral to a home health agency for a home safety evaluation and an Allen Cognitive Level Screen. The latter gives detailed information on how many hours of care the elder is anticipated to require per day. The home health agency will send physical and occupational therapists to the home to make recommendations on how to make the home safer and more accessible. Most Medicare plans cover the cost of these visits.

Medical-Care Management

The ROI mentioned above allows the CM to be fully involved with the medical care of the elder. One ROI form is usually completed for each health care entity associated with the elder—from doctors to insurance companies. Once the ROIs are in place with each health care entity, the care manager can take over any or all tasks related to the medical needs of the elder. These include:

- **Scheduling medical appointments:** The care manager schedules and attends all important medical appointments. It is also helpful for the companion who is working the shift on that day to attend the appointment, as they might be able to answer some questions better than the CM, because they are with the elder 24/7. Prior to the appointment, the care manager should ask the health care representative and the care team if they have any questions or concerns regarding the elder's health that should be addressed during the appointment. All appointments should be entered on the shared online calendar that is accessed by the entire home care team.

- **Coordinating regular medical care:** The CM keeps track of when the elder needs to see various providers, including regular dental care, eye exams, physicals, mammograms, or other annual medical tests. At times, medical care can get complicated, and it is the care manager's job to make sure appointments occur in a timely and coordinated fashion. Medical visits can be stressful for elders with dementia, so it is important to spread the visits out whenever possible.

- **Communicating with the family/health care representative (HCR):** It is the role of the care manager to discuss treatment recommendations with the family or the designated HCR (the person who makes medical decisions), so they can make informed decisions regarding the care of the elder. For instance, if a doctor recommends a surgery, the care manager gathers information regarding the options, such as the pros and cons of having the surgery, the risks, the alternatives, what the recovery is expected to be like, and so forth. The care manager then brings this information to the HCR, so they can make an informed decision on how they would like the elder's care to proceed.

- **Keeping medical records:** It is the care manager's job to keep records of the medical appointments and document what was discussed. The CM takes notes during the appointment and disseminates the information to the elder's HCR after the visit but before reporting to the rest of the home care team. The care manager must communicate medication changes to whoever is filling the medication boxes and remind the doctor to send orders for the change.

- **Advocating for the elder:** At times, it is necessary to advocate for the elder if the CM feels the elder is not getting the proper care or treatment or their needs are not being fully addressed. The CM brings any concerns to the family or HCR first for discussion. The CM then proceeds by taking action. An example would be if the elder was complaining about a new pain in some part of their body. The doctor may prescribe over-the-counter pain medicine, which is fine as a first defense. If that does not treat the pain within a few days, the CM might reach out to the doctor to request further treatment, perhaps an appointment or a referral. Since appointments can be hard to come by quickly, the CM needs to remain diligent in getting the elder seen sooner rather than later, perhaps by an alternative provider.

- **Becoming the elder's HCR:** In cases where the family or another person close to the elder is not continually available, some care managers are willing to take on the role of health care representative. It is essential that this decision and paperwork take place while the elder still has the capacity or understanding of what they are doing by agreeing to nominate the care manager as their health care representative. Doctors' offices often have advance directive forms available, or an elder law attorney can complete the paperwork. Forms are also available online, but forms may differ per state, so be sure to include the elder's state in your search. The HCR has the authority to make health care decisions for the elder, and the form goes into effect when the elder loses the ability to make decisions for themself.

- **Advance directives:** One of the first orders of business for the care manager is to make sure an advance directive for health care is in place. This form designates whom the elder wants to nominate as their health care representative (HCR) if they are no longer able to express their wishes or needs. It details the kinds of measures they want taken and under what circumstances. It is important to have these decisions made before the elder's disease is too advanced. Most states also have a form called a POLST or the portable orders for life-sustaining treatment. The elder or their representative fills out this form with the primary care doctor and designates how they would like emergency personnel to respond if they are found unresponsive. If an elder feels strongly that they would not like to be resuscitated, this is an important document to have completed. In Oregon, the information is entered into a database that emergency responders can access. In other states, emergency officials recommend hanging this bright-pink form in a place where it can be visible to emergency responders who are trained to look for it on the front of the refrigerator.

Home-Care Management

The care manager can be instrumental in working with the family to hire, schedule, train, and supervise companions. As mentioned above, some states do not allow a CM to solely manage this part of the elder's care without becoming a registered home care agency. (Refer to your state's Health Authority for rules.) If the state in which the elder lives will allow the CM to manage these tasks, it can be a significant relief to the family. Either way, the tasks listed below demonstrate how to get companions on board to take care of an elder, whether the CM is acting as a coach/assistant or managing the entire process. While the endeavor may appear somewhat daunting, once the team of companions is in place, it is worth every minute of the effort required to lay the groundwork. The family is able to maintain a better semblance of their daily lives independent of their elder, while knowing they are being tended to with the highest quality care, whether it is a few hours a day or around-the-clock care.

+ **Finding companions:** Candidates can be found among people currently working with the elder in some capacity (such as friends), or people recommended by family and friends. You can also search sites like www.Care.com, www.Nextdoor.com, www.Craigslist.com, and www.Indeed.com. Many people are leery of using Craigslist, and while it is important to vet applicants carefully—no matter what site is used—the Purple Nest Home Care Model found Craigslist to be the most successful site in finding good companions. That said, the Purple Nest found personal references to be, by far, the best resource for superb companions.

- **Interviewing candidates:** The first contact should be by phone, FaceTime, or Zoom. During this interview, you will want to cover a number of subjects: the applicant's availability and whether they have the interest and flexibility in their schedule to work the required shifts. (As a side note, if the need is for 24/7 care, it is necessary to hire three to four companions who are able to work one to three 24-hour shifts per week. If only a few hours a day or week are required, then one or two companions is likely sufficient.) During the interview it is important to gauge the prospective applicant's interest and passion for caregiving, how they feel about working on a team and taking direction, and whether they seem to be a good fit with the elder in terms of their personality. Are they going to enjoy spending several days a week with the elder? If they have prior caregiving experience, that is a bonus, but it is not necessary. Some companions hired for Lucy had experience with caring for their own family members in the past but had never worked as a companion/caregiver professionally. It is necessary, however, that the applicant be physically able to do the job, so be clear about those aspects of the position. (See the Sample Interview Questions for Companion Position on the Printable Documents page on our website, www.ThePurpleNest.net.)

- **Reaching out to the applicants' references:** Questions to ask references include how they rate the prospective candidate on honesty, patience, trustworthiness, and dependability. Also, ask if they work well with other people and are willing to take direction. If they have prior caregiving experience, ask what their rapport with the elder in their care was like. The best references will be previous supervisors and coworkers.

- **Conducting a face-to-face interview:** It is best to meet at a location close to the elder's house such as a coffee shop or restaurant, so if the interview goes well, the candidate can meet the elder afterward. The more the atmosphere can remain relaxed, the better. Interviewing someone who will be taking care of a person with dementia is far different than interviewing someone for, say, a customer service position. Coming into a private home and living with a person a few days a week is a unique and very personal situation. It is important to see who the "real" person is as much as possible. It's also important to tell the candidate about any challenging aspects of the position and characteristics or behaviors of the elder. How will they deal with those? Give them plenty of time to speak and ask questions.

- **Introducing the candidate to the elder:** If the face-to-face interview goes well, then it's time to take the candidate to meet the elder at their residence. This should last at least an hour to begin gauging the kind of rapport the prospective companion and elder may be able to have. If at least one companion has already been hired, then that person will likely also be present. They should act as a host by having some light refreshments or tea available. If the family is the party conducting the interview, they may want to invite the care manager to join the group, as the CM will have valuable insights into what to look for in a companion. As mentioned above, the atmosphere should be relaxed and more like a visit than an interview. At some point, allowing the elder to give a tour of their home is a good way to encourage interaction between the elder and the prospective candidate. The elder should be told why this person is here: that they are interested in joining the team who comes and stays with them. Once the candidate has left, it's good to immediately get a feel from the elder for how they felt about the person. The family can also get feedback from the care manager and companion if either or both were present. If another interview is called for, that is perfectly fine, as the goal is to hire a companion who will work out for a long period of time.

- **Finalizing the hiring activities and paperwork:** Once the candidate has been accepted by the family and elder, they should receive a copy of the Home Care Companion Handbook that lists the full details of the job. (See the template Home Care Companion Handbook on the Printable Documents page on our website.) This handbook is an important tool, which the newly hired companion should read in its entirety. The companion should initial each page and return the handbook to the hiring agent; a copy of the handbook should also be given to the new hire to keep for themself. The new hire must fill out several documents, including a contract and a background check (see the Companion Checklist at the end of Chapter 6). These documents should all be sent home with the candidate, so they can read them thoroughly. Once the candidate has completed the paperwork and the background check comes back clear, the care team can establish a start date. At this time, the newly hired companion should receive the Addendum, which lists emergency contacts and so forth. A current copy of the Home Care Companion Handbook and Addendum should be kept in a binder in the companions' bedroom for quick and easy access.

- **Training the companion:** How much training is required should be determined on a case-by-case basis, and it may change as the elder's dementia progresses. In the earlier stages of dementia, it may not take many sessions to bring a new companion up to speed. Much of the training will be on the job, but new hires should get at least two to three training sessions of approximately four hours each with the person who is training them. If there are already companions working for the elder, they are probably the best ones to train a new companion. If possible, it may behoove the new person to train with more than one companion and, of course, the family can provide training as well. The advice from a care manager is helpful to make sure all training topics are covered. (See the training criteria detailed in the Home Care Companion Handbook template on our website's Printable Documents page.)

Ongoing Management of Companions

The family may ask the care manager to aid in the scheduling of companions. As mentioned previously, some states may not allow the care manager to be directly involved in the scheduling process without being registered as an agency; in other words, some states may want the CM to only advise the family on how to go about creating the schedule for the companion team. As discussed in Chapter 6, you can configure the schedule a couple of different ways with 24-hour, 48-hour, or 72-hour shifts as well as different shift start/end times. (You can download sample schedules on the Printable Documents page of our website.)

When it comes to managing the care of the elder, it is extremely important that the CM can communicate with the companions on a variety of topics to make sure the elder is getting the highest quality of care. The following paragraphs offer helpful tips to effectively communicate with and supervise the team of companions.

- **Communication:** The care manager and home care team will be in frequent communication via text, email, or other method. How much time is spent communicating with each other can vary drastically depending on the stability of the elder. During times when a lot is going on with the health of the elder, the CM should save up notes and send all the information in one email so as not to overwhelm the companions with multiple messages. The CM should be cognizant and balance the need for sending out information and respecting the free time of the companions, as they will often be receiving email updates outside their working hours. For this reason, we suggest the companions be given at least an extra half hour of pay per month to compensate them for time working outside of their shifts. As mentioned, the companions handwrite their notes on printed pages in a binder or record their notes online in a Google doc about notable events, behaviors, or significant changes observed during the day concerning the elder. At the end of each shift—if using handwritten notes in a binder—the pages are photographed and sent via email or text to the care manager. The CM can disseminate the most pertinent information to the family or health care representative unless they wish to read all the daily notes. The CM always conveys any concerning information in the notes to the family and, quite possibly, to the appropriate member of the medical team.

- **Supervision:** When appropriate, or as allowed by law, the care manager can provide one-on-one supervision of the companions. One constructive practice is to hold one half-hour meeting per month with each companion. During this time the CM and companion can talk about any issues or concerns regarding the elder or perhaps even with another companion. This meeting can take place in person, over the phone, or on a Zoom call. The companion should be paid for this meeting time. It is also important for the care team to feel that they have an advocate and a resource to go to at any time for advice or support and that the care manager is available outside of the scheduled half hour on an as-needed basis. The CM may help resolve conflicts between the elder and a companion or between companions. A mediation meeting can be handled over the phone, in an online video chat, or in person, whichever is appropriate for the issue at hand. If the elder needs to discuss a conflict, the conversation would likely need to be in person or on video, as dementia patients are often challenged by telephone conversations, particularly in the middle to later stages of the disease.

- **Disciplinary action:** Occasionally it is necessary to take disciplinary action concerning a companion. This could be for a variety of reasons, such as being habitually late for their shift or having continued strife with members of the care team or the elder. Perhaps they made a minor ethical breach that doesn't rise to the level of termination but still requires a response. In these cases, it is necessary for whoever is managing the care team, whether it is the family or the CM, to call a meeting with the companion, outline the missteps, and make a plan of action. It may be helpful to have another member of the care team (perhaps the daily money manager but *not* another companion) attend the meeting. Afterward, notes of the meeting should be sent via email to all parties involved. The companion should acknowledge that they received the notes and that they agree with the assessment and follow-up plan. The care manager or family should print this email reply and place it in the companion's file.

- **Workers' Compensation or Unemployment:** Sometimes it is necessary to assist the companions in completing a workers' compensation or unemployment claim. If a companion is hurt on the job, the care manager or family member must fill out a portion of the workers' compensation claim. The CM or family member may also be asked to fill out a portion of an unemployment claim after the departure of a companion, although the daily money manager would handle most of the paperwork for these tasks if a DMM is working with the elder.

- **Monitoring home visits:** The care manager will make monthly visits or more frequently, if necessary, to assess how things are going for the elder and the care team. These visits are best unscheduled, so the CM can get an accurate picture of what is going on in the home. The CM should speak individually to the elder and the companion. The CM wants to know how the elder is feeling about their care and their companion or caregiver on duty. The care manager should visit during the shifts of all the different companions, so they can see the condition of the home and observe the dynamics between the elder and each companion. The CM should also speak individually with each companion and ask them how they are doing, how the work is going, how the elder is doing, and if there are any unmet needs or concerns to be addressed. The CM then relays these concerns to the family and works to address them.

If the care manager is responsible for all the above tasks, it puts them in the delicate position of representing both the interests of the elder and the companions. Making sure the companions are happy, being treated fairly, and compensated well are all concerns of the care manager. Furthermore, the CM is both an advocate for the elder and for the companions, and this is an important aspect of the job. The overarching goal of the CM in this specific scenario should be to build a loving, kind, dedicated, and content team for the purpose of creating superb quality of life for the elder. Creating a great team results in stability for everyone involved. As previously mentioned, the home care team employed for Lucy averaged well over two years and ended due to Lucy's health, not due to voluntary discharge. This is ultimately the best-case scenario for any elder.

The Cost of Hiring a Care Manager
An article on www.AARP.org, titled "Geriatric Care Managers Advocate for Older Adults—and Their Caregivers," gives several points to consider when hiring a care manager. They include the credentials and licenses of the CM, how long they have been practicing, their hourly rate, communication style, availability, and flexibility. The family should request references and thoroughly vet potential care managers.

In general, care managers are master's level social workers or nurses, and according to AARP, the cost for services ranges between $90 and $250 per hour. This usually includes travel time, phone calls, and paperwork. The fees may be higher or lower in any given city or state, so it is essential to research the costs in your location. Also, care management is not covered by medical insurance, Medicare, or usually by long-term care insurance. In cases of dementia, the family can expect a CM to be engaged in working for the elder anywhere from three to fifteen hours per month, depending on the needs and intensity of a given month. For instance, circumstances such as an acute illness or surgery would push the number of hours higher.

While the care manager should have clear latitude to make many decisions surrounding the care of the elder, if the family is the legal health care representative, they are ultimately responsible for the health care decisions. The parties should iron out the separation of decision-making up front, so there are no gray areas. For example, the CM is responsible for making medical appointments for the elder, and many appointments are regular maintenance visits with the dentist, eye doctor, and so forth that the family would not necessarily have to be involved in. On the other hand, if an emergency arises and the companion called the care manager to report it, the CM would, in turn, contact the family to inform them or request direction. The family, along with the advance directives set forth while the elder was able to instruct them, have final say in critical medical situations.

The Care Manager in a Legal Guardian Role

If it is within their purview and expertise, a care manager may take on the role of legal guardian. A legal guardian is a court-appointed person who is responsible for making medical and housing decisions. A guardian is necessary when an elder lacks capacity and has not already designated someone as their health care representative. A guardian is also sometimes necessary when the health care representative (HCR) is at odds with the elder, and the elder is refusing services that are necessary for their health and welfare. If no family or friend is able or willing to take on the role of the guardian, professional guardians also exist. Sometimes it is also necessary to designate a conservator, who manages a person's money if no durable power of attorney has been assigned.

The tasks of a guardian relevant to setting up a home care team are similar to those of a care manager. The legal guardian can perform these tasks or hire a care manager to perform these tasks. The tasks are similar except that the guardian does not have to consult with family or the HCR to make decisions, as the guardian has effectively become the HCR. The guardian also takes over some of the family's role, such as coordinating financial needs with the daily money manager or bookkeeper. While the guardian is not responsible for day-to-day finances, they would inform the bookkeeper about the cost of all medical expenses.

The family or concerned party should consult with an elder law attorney to start the legal process of guardianship. The elder law attorney can make referrals to professional guardians, as well as help vet a prospective guardian. If the family is available, ideally, they remain involved and make sure the guardian's choices are in the best interest of the elder. Again, the best strategy is to avoid the necessity of a guardian and to designate an HCR while the elder is still in the early stages of dementia. If this is not possible, putting the elder into the capable hands of a reputable guardian is the only remaining solution.

Whether or not a family or an elder decides to hire a care manager for ongoing services, it is beneficial to at least consult with a reputable CM as soon as possible at the start of the process of setting up the home for 24/7 care. A knowledgeable care manager can get this complex process off to a great start.

Care Manager Checklist

This checklist helps the care manager or the elder's family set up a comprehensive system for remain-at-home, medical-care management. Note: If you compare the Family Checklist to the following checklist, you can see that utilizing a care manager will take quite a bit of the burden off the family. It is best if the tasks listed below can be completed within the first one to two months after hiring the CM. We suggest dating each item as completed. (You can download this checklist from our website on the Printable Documents page.)

Assessment of the elder and their home:		
1		Interview the elder for their social and medical history. From the elder's perspective, what are their needs and goals for care? (See the sample Care Manager Intake Form on our website on the Printable Documents page.)
2		Interview members of the family and others familiar with the elder for social and medical history. From the family members' perspectives, what are the needs and goals for care?
3		Tour the elder's home to identify potential safety issues, evaluate the requirement for any special equipment, assess possible decluttering needs, and check the accommodations for companions.
Medical-care management and what is required to fulfill this role:		
4		Have the elder or the elder's representative sign a release of information (ROI) form in order to speak to the medical team.
5		Gather a list of all current medical diagnoses, medications (including supplements), and hospitalizations.
6		Contact the medical team (for example, primary care, specialists, dentists, eye doctors) and see which appointments have already been scheduled or still need to be scheduled. Make required appointments and post on an online calendar.

7		Verify the current medication list with the primary care provider. At each medical appointment with any member of the medical team the provider must check the medication list. Specialists may be prescribing medications, and these doctors will want to know what the elder is taking to safeguard against interactions.
8		Gather important information from the family and the elder's medical team, such as allergies, dietary restrictions, food preferences, and so forth. The list should contain any condition the companion team must be aware of and be included in the Home Care Companion Handbook. (See the template on our website on the Printable Documents page.)
9		Gain access to the elder's electronic medical records. If the elder and the family are willing, it is helpful to have the login information for the elder's electronic medical records, often called "MyChart" or a variation of this. From the electronic chart, the CM can see which medications are prescribed, leave messages for the doctor regarding health concerns, make or change appointments, and even upload pictures of possible concerns, for example, a new skin rash.

CHAPTER 8
Branch Five: The Daily Money Manager

The daily money manager (DMM) assists the elder and their family with all *non-care-related tasks*, such as any task related to the client's finances, bills, and tax preparation; their personal home and any other properties; and all other non-care-related professional requirements. These could include working with long-term care insurance processors, tax preparers, insurance agents, attorneys, home-repair contractors, grounds maintenance companies, house-cleaning companies, and any other need that requires hiring a specific professional. The DMM keeps the client's financial records, pays bills, and helps find companies for non-care services.

The elder or their family can decide which of these tasks they want to hire a DMM to take care of and which ones they will take care of themselves. Much depends on the complexities of the elder's estate. For instance, if the estate consists of only the home the elder lives in, managing the elder's finances will be less involved, but if the estate has other properties, such as rentals, having a qualified DMM can save the family a lot of time, energy, and quite possibly money. Furthermore, the DMM must maintain confidentiality about the elder's health condition, finances, and all personal information concerning the elder and their family.

NOTES

Finding a Daily Money Manager

How much a particular family needs or wants a person in the DMM role depends on several factors. In Lucy's case, the family did not live in the same state as the elder and had a busy career and young family. Thus, Lucy's family chose to rely heavily on the DMM to take care of the elder's business affairs, which included rental properties. That said, even private homes are a little like "needy children who never grow up and leave," so the home often needs ongoing repairs or updates. There are two advantages to maintaining and possibly even updating the main residence: first, the home is kept safe and comfortable for the elder, and second, when it comes time to sell the home it will be more market ready. Spreading the tasks out over a few years, perhaps tackling two to four projects per year, can help budget-wise (and energy-wise).

When searching for someone to fill the DMM role, you can look for applicants under the categories of daily money manager (although this term is still rather new for most people), bookkeeper, professional organizer, or personal assistant. That said, people with these credentials may not provide all the services a daily money manager does, so it might be necessary to hire more than one person to meet your elder's needs. Often, any of these professionals can provide references for tasks or projects they do not offer themselves.

A few different ways exist to find a DMM. One is on a website for The American Association of Daily Money Managers at www.AADMM.com. Another good resource is the National Association of Productivity and Organizing Professionals at www.NAPO.net. With so many possible websites to find someone to fill the DMM role, it's good practice to look at the ratings of a site and read personal reviews when available. (We have links to reputable websites to find personal assistants, bookkeepers, and other service providers on the Resources page on our website, www.ThePurpleNest.net.)

The Daily Money Manager's Task Details

When a DMM is starting out with a new client, they must assess several important items. First, where is the elder cognitively? Are they capable of making their own decisions, or will the family be making decisions on behalf of the elder? In the earlier stages of dementia, many elders will not relinquish any control to their adult children or other family members. This can be challenging if the elder is not really taking care of business but thinks they are.

Ideally, the elder has already signed a durable power of attorney (DPOA), so the DMM can work directly for the person who has the power of attorney. While the absence of a DPOA does not exclude the DMM from performing their duties, it is extremely helpful if the elder has previously shared that power with someone else. The DMM may (with *may* being the operative word) be able to help facilitate this if the family has reached an impasse in getting their elder to sign the DPOA. That said, the elder may have signed the DPOA and not given control of their affairs over to their family members but perhaps given control to a friend or even an outside professional. A DPOA in and of itself does not relinquish the elder's decision-making power. That change may come down the road when a professional can assess whether the elder is no longer capable of making financial decisions. For all these reasons, dealing with an elder who has dementia can be challenging.

Next, the DMM assesses if the family needs help with the tasks they are taking care of themselves. Some families are more ready than others to let go of the business affairs they are currently in charge of. Others are grateful to turn over *all* their elder's business cares to someone else. The DMM's ability to establish trust with both the elder and the family is extremely important. Family members are often burned out by the time a DMM comes along, and they are ready to hand over the reins for the elder's many financial tasks, including tax preparation, paying utility bills, making mortgage payments, addressing medical statements and bills, and staying on top of other monthly and annual financial obligations. All DMM applicants should provide ample references to help the elder and their circle of support feel reassured.

Assessing whether the finances are organized can be straightforward, or it can be a complex maze, particularly if the financial documents are in disarray, which is highly likely. The first goal of the DMM is to organize the elder's papers and create a filing system or become familiar with the system that existed previously. The DMM addresses everything from back taxes to current taxes, though they usually involve a CPA or tax preparer to make sure everything is covered. The DMM sets up a bookkeeping system to utilize going forward or updates an existing system. Once this is all in order, the DMM usually gets as many regular bills set up for autopay as possible. This includes accounts such as utilities, mortgage, telephone, internet/cable, insurance policies, and so on. The DMM also makes any payments due to contractors hired for any variety of projects or repairs. These tasks alone are a huge load off whoever was taking care of them before bringing the DMM into the care team.

The DMM can be of great assistance with getting the home organized. If the DMM does not include this in their services, they can help the family find a professional organizer. A professional organizer takes charge of helping the elder and their family cull unwanted items and create organizational systems, not only for the main living area but also for storage units, garages, and outbuildings.

It is important to note that during the initial stages of organizing the papers in the elder's home, the DMM is often like a detective, trying to determine how various documents, scraps of papers, invoices, receipts, unusual bank entries, uncashed checks, and other miscellaneous papers fit into the elder's life. When an unusual piece of paper or bank entry crosses the daily money manager's path, they should not ignore these "breadcrumb trails." They can lead to investments or expenses previously unknown by the family, because the elder has not shared these items with their family and has forgotten these details. In Lucy's case, she had a $100,000 certificate of deposit (CD) that had matured at the bank and needed to be cashed in. However, Lucy no longer understood the meaning of a CD and kept throwing away the letters from the bank requesting action. Obviously, this was a nice surprise for Lucy's family.

The DMM can also find professionals to take on home repairs and safety updates, such as handrails, common locks on all doors, alarm systems, anti-slip treads on stairs, and so forth. (Chapter 9: Equipping the Home discusses a variety of items to make the home safe.)

Included in the task of getting the home in good order is setting up a bedroom for the companions. As a reminder, we discussed the details and essentials of this room in Chapter 3: Phases of Care, and they are included on the Family Checklist in Chapter 5. Again, the family can choose to take care of these tasks or assign them to the DMM or a professional organizer.

Below is a comprehensive list of the DMM's potential responsibilities for the elder and the family. The DMM can also research and aid in hiring other professionals such as a CPA, insurance agent, payroll company, estate attorney, and so on and oversee the big picture, similar to a project manager. While not everything listed may be required in all cases, just knowing someone can manage all these time-consuming tasks with multiple participants can be a great comfort to everyone involved. An elder who is trying to take care of even a few of these items may be more prone to "letting go" once they see how much this person can help them.

- **Finance/bookkeeping-related tasks:**

  - Prepare documents, receipts, and other important papers for the client's personal federal and state (and potentially local/city) tax returns, to be completed by a CPA or other tax professional.

  - Make estimated/quarterly tax payments for personal tax returns and payroll tax returns to the IRS and the state as advised by the elder's CPA.

  - Request quarterly payroll reports from the payroll company and provide to the CPA for quarterly preparation to both the IRS and the state (in most cases).

  - Pay the client's regular monthly bills (for example, utilities, phone, medical, mortgage, insurance, internet).

  - Set up bills on automatic payment wherever possible.

  - Process payroll for the long-term care insurance company (if applicable) to reimburse for payroll expenses (for the companions, not the CM or DMM).

  - Process the companions' payroll for the payroll company.

  - Create a budget with the family to stay within and prioritize additional costs and maintenance projects according to the agreed-upon parameters.

  - Review insurance policies. This review includes the homeowner's policy and, if applicable, the client may require an umbrella policy (personal and/or commercial) and an Employers Non-Ownership Liability (ENOL) policy, so the client and companions are fully insured when riding in a companion's car while the companion is working.

  - At least monthly, review the expenses coming out of the elder's accounts for any suspicious activity. This can mean keeping an eye out for fraud from possible online hacking or excessive, unapproved, or otherwise unusual spending by companions or unauthorized family members. Unexpected expenses don't always signify abuse so much as a new boundary needs to be discussed and established within the care team (for example, how often the companions can dine out and the limit to spend on house-related purchases before asking for permission).

- **Maintenance-related tasks:**

  - Find reputable vendors for the various maintenance, repairs, and home modifications for the client's changing needs in their home (for example, installation of a ramp and grab rails).

  - As required, contact carpenters, plumbers, electricians, landscapers, house cleaners, carpet cleaners, tree trimmers, pest management companies, chimney cleaners, and so forth to get bids, schedule the work, and pay invoices.

  - On occasion, for larger maintenance projects, the DMM may need to meet vendors at the client's home. For smaller projects, the companions can usually explain the issue at hand to the vendor.

- **Coordinating with other professionals or individuals:**

  - Contact a labor attorney to create an acceptable legal contract for the companions. Before a contract can be created, decisions must be made regarding the following:

    1. Whether the companions will be reimbursed for mileage while driving on-the-clock

    2. If companions will be paid any holiday pay, vacation pay, or sick pay (Note: Some states may require sick pay by law.)

    3. The rate of pay, both hourly (for training purposes, part-time contracting, and additional miscellaneous errands) and per each 24-hour shift

- Contact the payroll technician to process a new companion hire (submit Form I-9, Form W-4, direct-deposit form, and so forth).

- Familiarize companions with the payroll company's system to access pay stubs.

- Contact the workers' compensation processor if a companion gets hurt while on the job and files a claim.

- Respond to correspondence received when a companion files an unemployment claim.

- Respond to the payroll company and any respective parties when a companion has a garnishment to process.

- Communicate with companions as necessary, informing them of maintenance and home-related projects and schedules, payroll updates, requesting timesheets and mileage forms, and approving larger purchases for the client (if the budget is turned over to the DMM by the family).

The Cost of Hiring a Daily Money Manager

As illustrated, the number of responsibilities involved in maintaining the business and property of the elder is huge. The general pay range for a DMM is $75 to $125 per hour. Some professional organizers and daily money managers charge more than $125 per hour; some charge for travel time (either full or partial), and some charge by the minute, while others charge in six-minute or fifteen-minute increments.

While a long-term care insurance policy will not pay for the services of a DMM, if the elder does have a long-term care policy, it will pay the companions' wages up to the maximum amount of the policy. Therefore, the budget can be set as necessary, and tasks delegated to others. Many of the items listed above do not require a DMM, but isn't it good to know someone can take the load off a situation that may already be quite stressful? Dealing with dementia is a challenge in and of itself for everyone involved; the daily money manager is there should you need them to ease some of the strain.

The most important qualities of the individual filling this role are integrity, tenacity, curiosity, and an ability to think outside the box. Each client will likely have their own special needs that crop up unexpectedly that the DMM may not have dealt with before. Resourcefulness and a willingness to learn are great characteristics to look for in a DMM. Also, it is helpful if the DMM has a basic knowledge of Excel to help track projects. If the DMM has access to QuickBooks, that is also helpful but not required.

For a DMM who enters the realm of working with a person with dementia, it can be time-consuming, challenging, and sometimes frustrating and is absolutely, positively worth *every* ounce of energy and time that goes into creating a superb support system for both the elder and their family members! Everything the daily money manager does for the client now with their home, their legal matters, and so forth will help the entire family cope with the challenges of the present as well as ease into the transition of possible full-time assisted living or when the elder eventually passes on. The personal and professional rewards far outweigh the challenges.

Daily Money Manager Checklist

This list is intended to help the daily money manager (DMM) clarify and prioritize goals as they work to establish the Purple Nest Home Care Model in a new client's home. Remember that this position may be filled by someone with another title, such as a professional organizer or a personal assistant.

If you compare the following checklist with the Family Checklist in Chapter 5, you will see that utilizing a daily money manager can take a significant burden off the family. (You can download this checklist from our website on the Printable Documents page.)

We suggest dating each item as completed.

Establish an easy way to be able to pay the client's bills, considering the following:		
1		If using checks, can the client sign checks, and can you meet with them regularly?
2		Will a family member or other trusted party be writing checks instead of you?
3		It is legal to use a signature stamp if the elder/family decides that writing paper checks is the preferred method for paying bills. Most office supply stores or print shops can make a signature stamp for a reasonable price. Let the family determine where to keep the signature stamp for safekeeping.
4		If you are writing the checks, establish rules with the family surrounding the processes you will follow, for example, the amount that requires preapproval by a family member and which family member provides approval.
5		Work with the person who has online access to the elder's bank account to set up an automatic bill paying system with the client's bank or the individual billing companies, such as utility and insurance companies. This can save a lot of time and effort over the long term.

6		Work with the family to determine how the companions will make purchases for everyday items, such as groceries, general merchandise, eating out, and attending functions. The receipts for all purchases are generally submitted to the DMM for review. Determine with the family which receipts they want to keep long term and how and where to store them.
7		Establish an efficient system to get bills and other important mail from the client, including bank statements. It is helpful to have the bank statement available online and to include images of the checks written, especially if carbon checks are not used. Banks often charge a minimal monthly fee for this service, but it's worth its weight in gold! Some ways to collect the important mail include picking it up periodically at the client's home, or perhaps the companions can mail it to you in bulk. Bills that are on autopay can be shredded by companions while others that have due dates to pay by check or online can be texted to you by the companions, especially if the bills are time sensitive. The companions can collect these types of bills throughout the month and place them in an envelope for you, along with the receipts from purchases for the month.
Find a reputable payroll company licensed in the state where the elder lives. There are numerous payroll-related tasks, such as:		
8		Determining the frequency of pay for the companions
9		Determining the time-tracking process for submitting payroll
10		Having companions complete direct-deposit paperwork with the payroll company
11		Working with the client's CPA or tax preparer to complete various payroll-related forms that the payroll company does not complete (The tax laws for companionship are different than for other business types.)
12		Establishing regular reimbursement payments to the elder for the companions' wages if the elder has a long-term care insurance policy (This is required, because the elder pays each payroll upfront and is then reimbursed afterward.)

	Become familiar with the following documentation:	
13		Get a digital copy of the DPOA. Even though you likely won't be listed in the DPOA, it's helpful to have this document on file.
14		Secure a copy of the Home Care Companion Handbook (this contains important guidelines that the DMM should be aware of) and the Addendum (this contains important contact information).
15		Secure a copy of the companions' sample contract, which will list details concerning any paid holidays, sick pay, vacation pay, and so forth.
16		Gain access to the care team's online calendar, so you are informed of medical appointments, classes, in-home services, or other activities that might require payment or reimbursement.

CHAPTER 9
Equipping the Home

This chapter focuses on ways to keep a person who has dementia safe in their home in response to common behaviors that may arise during the progression of the disease. Addressing a wide variety of safety concerns is at the top of all lists when it comes to making sure an elder remains as free from harm as possible while remaining in their own home. Even if someone, such as a companion, is with the elder 24/7, they cannot keep an eye on the elder every minute of every day.

Though we should never think of an elder with dementia as "childish" or "childlike," when it comes to making the home safe for them, some of the equipment used is similar to the equipment used when childproofing a home. Some products have even been designed specifically for people with dementia. A few particularly useful products include alarms, gates, GPS technology, AirTags, and monitors to keep track of the elder at all times, especially when challenging behaviors present themselves.

Alarms, Locks, ID Bracelets, and "Sunflowers"

One example of a challenging behavior is wandering, which means the elder leaves the house and walks around the neighborhood, sometimes to a familiar place and other times during a disoriented state with no clear destination in mind. Wandering can be a common behavior during the middle and late stages of dementia. A helpful solution is door alarms, which are affordable, easy to install, easily turned on and off with remote controls, and LOUD! We recommend placing an alarm on every

NOTES

outside door. To help a person who forgets easily, it is wise to print out simple signs to put on the doors that remind them the alarm will go off if they open the door. A simple red hexagonal "STOP" sign is a great symbol to remind the elder not to open the door before seeking help. (See the sample door alarm signs on the Printable Documents page on our website at www.ThePurpleNest.net.)

Replacing regular doorknobs with locking doorknobs is an easy solution, but we recommend choosing the kind where a common key can open multiple doorknobs, alleviating the necessity to keep track of several keys.

To be proactive regarding wandering, it's always a good idea to get an ID bracelet for a person with dementia before (or if) the behavior presents itself. The bracelets are made to be difficult to remove and have the elder's name and phone number on them. You can put any information desired on them, such as if the elder has a medical condition, like a seizure disorder. For an individual who is particularly prone to wandering, several GPS products are available. You can even put one inside their shoes! Plus, you can choose from a variety of watches and other gadgets for them to wear.

The Alzheimer's Store (www.AlzStore.com) has a great selection of these kinds of products, which includes alarms that can be activated if the elder gets up in the middle of the night, motion detectors, and more. For traveling, you can purchase a "hidden disabilities sunflower," which is worn around the neck on a lanyard to cue people that the elder may need some additional help. These are popular in Europe and are just beginning to emerge in the United States. (See the sample on the Resources page on our website.)

Some homes may require locks on gates as well. If the home has an outdoor seating area where the elder enjoys hanging out or eating meals, the companion needs to be able to leave them periodically for brief moments to go inside. Dementia patients who are determined to wander can be clever about it and take advantage of such moments to make a dash to start roaming. Therefore, it is essential to have locks on all garden gates as well.

If the gate must be accessible and lockable on both sides for reasons such as allowing yard service workers to gain access when no one is home, you can install keyed locks or long-chained padlocks. Choose a good place to hide the key or get a lockbox for both sides of the gate. This can be handy if a companion gets locked out of the house, something not out of the realm of possibilities. The elder could accidentally lock a companion out, for instance, if they see the door open and lock it to feel safe. For this reason, it is a good idea to also have a lockbox on the property with a key to the house. This will allow contractors or cleaning services to access the home if the elder and companion are away during the time work is being done. The noise of repair work and cleaning is upsetting to some dementia patients, so leaving during those times is usually better for everyone.

In addition, the Alzheimer's Association coordinates a national service called "24/7 Wandering Support for a Safe Return." To take advantage of this service the family signs up online and pays a monthly membership fee. When an incident occurs, a call goes into MedicAlert's Emergency Response Team. They collect all the information and generate a missing-person report to local police, emergency medical services, and other authorities as appropriate. MedicAlert follows up on the case until it is resolved. The service already has all the details about the elder, including other medical conditions that would be important for authorities to know. If all other tactics have failed, this service could provide the best solution.

The Nitty-Gritty on Gates

It's good practice to block all stairways in the elder's home as well as rooms where items best kept out of reach are stored. Some "child gates"—or even "pet gates"—are more substantial than others. Choose one that cannot be knocked down too easily, yet not too difficult to knock down in the event of a fire and the need to escape quickly together.

You can add difficulty to opening a gate by attaching a bicycle chain and lock around the bottom of the gate. The companion might only put on this chain and lock during the night, for example, to keep an elder from going downstairs on their own while the companion is sleeping.

"Baby" Monitors

One of the most important pieces of safety equipment to purchase for nighttime is a set of baby monitors. This simple instrument is useful around the house for a variety of scenarios, but we highly recommend having a set for sleeping hours. The volume can be kept low enough in the companion's room to—hopefully—not keep them awake should the elder snore loudly. If the elder does snore, the companion can place the monitor away from their bedside table.

If the elder gets up in the night to use the bathroom, the companion may or may not hear this, especially if there is a commode in the bedroom (which is a good idea during the later stages of dementia). One helpful idea is to put a trail of newspapers down from the bed to the commode. The sound of their footsteps will come through the monitor, as well as catching an "accident" should it occur on the way to the commode. Ultimately, each companion must figure out the best volume for the baby monitor that allows them to sleep but also allows them to hear if an emergency arises.

Floor Alarm Pads and Motion Sensor Alarms

Another possible solution for nighttime safety is an alarm pad placed on the floor next to the bed, so when their feet hit the floor the alarm goes off. However, some elders may find the alarm startling and have trouble going back to sleep. In some cases, these alarms have even caused falls. When possible, find alternatives such as motion detectors that only sound an alarm in the companion's room and not in the elder's room. (See the link to a sample monitor that can be placed under the bed or on a nightstand on the Resources page on our website.) A wide variety of products are available, so with some good research, you should be able to find a solution for any given situation.

Handrails and Anti-Slip Treads

Handrails are another essential addition to the home. Chances are that some may have already been installed in or near an elder's bathtub or shower, but if not, it's time to do so. With the advancement of dementia, balance issues will increase; therefore, being proactive can ward off a fall. Having short handrails next to toilets is helpful as well.

If the house has stairs leading to upper bedrooms, having strong, well-anchored rails on both sides is very important. Additionally, be sure to place anti-slip treads on all wooden stairs, both inside and outside the home. Experts in this field recommend transparent anti-slip treads for inside stairs and neon-edged anti-slip treads for outside stairs.

Helpful Kitchen Items

Allowing an elder to help in the kitchen can give them a sense of purpose and satisfaction, especially if they were avid cooks in their younger years; not allowing them to help in the kitchen could be difficult for them. Using a set of cutting gloves allows them to continue helping cut vegetables when safety is a concern. At some point, from a coordination perspective, using cutting gloves may no longer be possible, so companions can find other ways for the elder to help, such as measuring ingredients and stirring. Of course, being at the stove is not advisable if an elder isn't up to the task.

As with any activity, companions should be ready for a change in capabilities on an ongoing basis. What is perfectly fine to allow today could change tomorrow; it is, unfortunately, the nature of dementia. Likewise, not being able to do something one day might not mean they cannot do that same thing just fine many times afterward, so completely ceasing an activity an elder enjoys should be thoughtfully and thoroughly vetted.

Using appliances is likely another area of concern for people with dementia. We suggest the family purchase a mechanically based microwave, because it is not digital and only has one or two knobs to turn to select the time and function desired. This helps prevent overcooking or burning the food or even causing a fire in the microwave. You may need to visit a restaurant supply store to find this type of microwave.

Another appliance you might want to bring into the kitchen is an electric kettle, which avoids using the stovetop to heat water for tea and hot chocolate or when making instant meals. Most fires that occur in the homes of persons with dementia happen from stovetop cooking, so finding gadgets that eliminate the need to use the stove is a good idea, especially if the elder is still living on their own without 24/7 companionship. In this case, it might be a good idea for the companions to unplug the stove when they leave and the elder will be alone.

Hot water can be another source of concern in the kitchen, in the shower or tub, or at any faucet the elder uses. You can choose from a wide variety of hot/cold labels that easily attach to the wall or directly to the handles.

A Few Final Recommendations

The home should have adequate heating and air conditioning, not only for the elder's preferences but for the companions' preferences as well. Space heaters and window air conditioning units should be provided, if necessary.

Putting together an emergency kit for power outages and natural disasters is always a good idea, which would include firewood if the home has a wood-burning stove or fireplace. It's important to include at least two weeks' worth of medications in the emergency kit, though this should be updated at a minimum of every six months or as recommended by a physician or pharmacist.

As mentioned, a home health agency can come to the home and go through the entire house to evaluate whether any safety issues exist. The person conducting the assessment might tape the walls to indicate where grab bars should go in the bathroom. They are also likely to advise the care team to remove throw rugs, as they can be tripping hazards. Also, they can recommend safety equipment, such as toilet risers, shower benches, transfer poles, and railings.

Finally, one more item that can be useful is a large-face digital clock that displays the time, day of the week, and date. People with dementia tend to lose the ability to judge time and track the date, so having one in the main living quarters and one in the elder's bedroom can help them significantly.

The suggestions in this chapter are not meant to be complete, as countless products are available that could be right for the individual and their care management team. (You can find links to many of the products mentioned in this chapter on the Resources page on our website.) The most important way to make a home safe is to be as thorough as possible and ready to implement something new as the need arises.

CHAPTER 10
Common Behaviors of People with Dementia

We at the Purple Nest are not medical practitioners, nor dementia experts, however, in this chapter, we will provide some of the common dementia behaviors you may encounter with your family member. As always, it is important that the people caring for a dementia patient seek out professional advice on specific behaviors, health conditions, and challenges as the needs arise. Great resources are available regarding the various behaviors people with dementia may display at some point during their illness and how to best address them. (We have listed several of these on the Resources page on our website at www.ThePurpleNest.net.)

Often, when a person is finally diagnosed with dementia, they have moved from the early stage of the disease, or the preclinical stage where they may not have had symptoms, to mild cognitive impairment (MCI). Some data shows the MCI stage lasting two to four years. During this time, the person with dementia is usually still fully capable of performing activities of daily living (ADLs) and may only require reminders on how to do certain things.

From MCI the individual advances to mild dementia. This is the stage where cognitive impairment really starts to become obvious through symptoms such as short-term memory loss, problem solving difficulty, and the misplacement of items.

During the moderate stage of dementia, the person will begin to have some difficulty with ADLs and greater judgment and memory issues. This stage can last

NOTES

two to four years. Eventually, the disease advances into the severe stage where the elder may lose awareness of their surroundings, their ability to communicate, and their ability to walk. This final stage may last one to two years. An article in *Medical News Today*, "How Long Does Dementia Last? Duration and Life Expectancy," chronicles the different stages of the most common forms of dementia, which includes Alzheimer's disease, Lewy body dementia, vascular dementia, and frontotemporal dementia.

Each type of dementia has different timelines and sometimes behaviors, so it is helpful to try to obtain an accurate diagnosis to provide the individual the best care possible. For the Purple Nest Home Care Model, the data given is associated with Alzheimer's disease. Some clinical evaluations consider there to be seven stages of dementia for Alzheimer's disease versus the four outlined here. (See the Reisberg Stages of Alzheimer's chart on the Resources page on our website.)

The *Medical News Today* article goes on to say that the average life expectancy for a person with dementia is about eight to ten years after they've received a diagnosis, and many times the diagnosis doesn't come right away, particularly if they had few symptoms during the preclinical stage. This means the person with dementia could conceivably remain in their own home for most of the eight to ten years, as long as they are well cared for. It is not common, but some people may live as many as fifteen to twenty years with the disease. Plus, there are other factors to take into consideration, such as the person's age when they are diagnosed with dementia.

In Lucy's case, she was cared for by a team of companions for almost five years, though she had been experiencing dementia-related symptoms for at least five years prior. Therefore, she remained in her own home until she entered the late stage of the disease. Of course, each individual progresses at their own speed with unique needs along the way. Information regarding Lucy's story is meant strictly to illustrate what is possible. Of course, there are no guarantees regarding how many years a person with dementia will be able to remain in their own home.

Hiding and Hoarding

One behavior a person with dementia can exhibit at some point is hiding or hoarding objects. Researchers in this field believe people with dementia do this to give themselves a sense of control or they may actually be looking for something but cannot remember what. Beyond the inconvenience of this behavior, it can be dangerous. It is extremely important to store toxic products in a place the elder cannot access. If possible, it's good to have a lockable room, drawer, or cabinet for cleaning supplies, important papers, checkbooks, jewelry, and other valuable items that are best kept out of reach. The family may want to keep the most valuable items locked away—such as heirlooms and jewelry—because these items can be easily misplaced. There may be pushback initially, if, for example, wedding rings are removed, but with dementia there is a good chance the elder will get past this initial frustration. If not, they may be capable of keeping track of the item, at least for the time being.

Another everyday item that can pose a problem is the trash. Having a good quality trash can that is more difficult to operate or keeping one under a cupboard with a childproof lock on the door can help avoid rummaging. We recommend checking the trash before taking it out if the elder regularly displays hiding or hoarding behaviors. If hoarding food is an issue, there might be one or two places where the individual is most prone to hiding those tidbits. It's a good idea to frequently check these common hoarding places to try to prevent ant or rodent infestations. If food hoarding becomes a real problem, you can keep food inside cupboards that lock and only bring it out when it's time to eat.

When an elder hides objects, the day can really be thrown out of whack. The elder may hide something they need in order to function, like dentures, eyeglasses, or hearing aids. Discovering that something essential has gone missing moments before leaving for an appointment can suddenly create chaos. Over time, the companion will find the elder's typical hiding places, but it adds to the argument for trying to keep the home minimally furnished and clutter-free. Good places to regularly check for hidden items are in clothes pockets (such as jackets, robes, or pants), under the bed, in dresser drawers, and in closet corners.

If the repeated loss of dentures or hearing aids is an issue, it may be best to only give the elder their dentures before meals and then store them the rest of the time. Similarly, if the elder's hearing loss is not too severe, you can give the elder their hearing aids only when required, for example, before a doctor's appointment or during visits with friends. You can purchase hearing aid clips that attach to the hearing aids and then go around the back of the neck and clip to clothing, so if the elder takes the hearing aids out, they are still attached to the elder's clothes.

One way to keep track of things the elder wants to hide or hoard is by providing a special personal place for them to put things like a drawer, cupboard, box, or trunk. They may need to be reminded of where that special place is from time to time or direct them to it, so they can enjoy some free time rummaging. Decorating and labeling the box can help as well.

NOTES

Some dementia patients are prone to throwing away or hiding mail, so getting a post office box, having most mail delivered to the home of a family member, having a locked mailbox, or just being on top of it when the mail comes can help avoid losing important correspondence.

Hallucinations, Delusions, Illusions, and Delirium

The definition of a hallucination is when a person hears, sees, smells, or has the feeling things are there that really are not. In other words, hallucinations are sensory perceptions without stimuli. The elder may tell the companion they can see a family member, possibly one who has passed away like a parent, spouse, or other relative. In Lucy's case, she believed her brother, (who was deceased) was next door visiting the neighbors. For several days she relayed this revelation every morning, because she liked to look out the window at the neighbor's house when she got up. She swore she saw her brother go into the house. There was a photo of her brother on the bureau next to the window, so a companion decided to remove it, and that particular behavior stopped. She could have been experiencing a hallucination, or it could have been a delusion; it is difficult to tell.

According to an article on www.UnitedWeCare.com, titled "Hallucinations, Delusions, Illusions, and Delirium: What's the Difference Between Them," delirium is an abrupt emotional change that causes mental confusion where a person may find it difficult to remain conscious, possibly falling asleep, or experiencing an emotional disturbance. Delerium is often caused by illness, infection, or medication change. Delerium is acute and reversable, so it's important not to ignore or minimize unusual behaviors, as the delirium might be easily treated.

Though similar, the difference between a delusion and an illusion is that an illusion is a distortion of the senses. For instance, the elder may see a rope and believe it's a snake. The definition of a delusion is when the person believes something is real when it is not, and this belief has a negative connotation. For example, Lucy believed some kind of social gathering was going on at the neighbor's house, and she felt slighted that she wasn't invited. Also, with delusions the elder may say there are people in other parts of the house. Another common delusion for people with dementia is that their spouse is cheating on them. Sometimes the elder cannot be talked out of their perceptions; other times they can through gentle repeated reassurances.

An online article by the Weill Institute for Neurosciences, titled "Medications and Dementia," emphasizes that treating the potential underlying causes of hallucinations or other forms of agitation discussed above is preferred over medications. Hallucinations and agitation can be due to infections, pain, side effects from medications, environmental factors, or social factors. The article goes on to suggest using nonpharmaceutical techniques as the first steps in shifting difficult behaviors:

- Create a calm, quiet environment that maintains personal comfort (for example, adjusting the lighting, temperature, and noise level).

- Have the person with dementia participate in physical therapy, music therapy, aquatic therapy, or other regularly scheduled activities.

- Address social factors and provide good communication skills, such as how to calmly talk to and engage the patient, for instance, when introducing them to new caregivers or routines.

We suggest monitoring the TV for violent or upsetting programs. It might be helpful to turn off the TV for a while or change the program. People with dementia can feel like the violent scene is happening right there in their living room. The local news can often be too disturbing for the elder. If they have a favorite show and it has some action scenes, it doesn't mean they cannot watch the show. The companion simply needs to use good judgment based on how the individual reacts.

These behaviors can be a real challenge for the family, companion, or caregiver to deal with, particularly when the elder becomes obsessed with an idea or belief and reiterates it multiple times throughout the day. The best ways to deal with these behaviors are agreement and distraction. Arguing or giving a person with dementia a "reality check" is not recommended.

Here are more suggestions that can help a companion or family member deal with an elder who is agitated:

- Try not to react when you get blamed for something.

- Don't argue with the person.

- Let the elder know they are safe.

- Give them a hug or gentle touch like rubbing their shoulders.

- Distract, distract, distract.

Distraction is one of the best ways to shift behavior. It could be as simple as changing the subject, moving to another room, going for a walk, or watching TV. One suggestion is to find videos on YouTube with beautiful scenery accompanied by music. Learning the elder's favorite music and then finding the corresponding videos to watch on TV or playing old CDs from their collection can also be effective in shifting the mood of a dementia patient when they are having a tough time.

A documentary made in 2014, called *Alive Inside*, illustrates the remarkable effects that music can have on people with even severe dementia. Some people went from a near comatose state into a very lucid state of mind when exposed to music they had enjoyed listening to in their past. (We have a link to this film on the Resources page on our website.)

Eventually, companions will find the kinds of activities that work for the elder in their care. While watching TV can be a good source to keep a person with dementia focused and entertained, it should not be a substitute for personal interaction, particularly for long periods of time.

Techniques taken from improvisational theater can be helpful when dealing with an elder who is experiencing delusions or hallucinations. When the elder expresses a deeply held delusion, try using the "Yes, and ..." technique used in improvisational theater. With this technique, you accept what the individual is saying, and you add to it. For example, in Lucy's case, when she believed her brother was next door, telling her that her brother was deceased and couldn't possibly be next door would be distressing and not helpful. Instead, we would say, "Yes, and we'll go check on that later after breakfast," thus stepping into her world. With dementia this can be enough to help them forget the thought for the rest of the day. Other times they may come back to it over and over throughout the day.

Sleep Issues and Sundowning

As mentioned, sundowning is when an elder experiences an increase in confusion, anxiety, agitation, pacing, and disorientation beginning late afternoon and often continuing throughout the night. Sundowning is a fairly common behavior in persons with dementia. The exact cause is unknown, but it is attributed to changes in the brain due to the disease. An article on the National Institute on Aging's (NIA) website, "Tips for Coping with Sundowning," gives several possible causes of sundowning as well as ways to cope with this challenge. One possible cause of sundowning is that the changes in the brain of a person with dementia affect a person's biological clock, leading to confused sleep-wake cycles. That said, there can be triggers to sundowning as well, and learning what an individual's triggers are can help to better manage the behavior.

Some of the conditions the NIA suggests contribute to sleep disturbances and sundowning are mental and physical exhaustion from a full day of activity, for example, when the elder may have struggled to keep up in an unfamiliar or overstimulating environment. Other factors that may cause sleep interruptions are shadows being cast on the bedroom walls, disorientation due to the inability to separate dreams from reality, and stressful or frustrating nonverbal behaviors of those around the elder. These are all causes that can be easily addressed by, for example, not letting the elder get too exhausted, lighting the home well in the afternoon and evening, having a low-glowing nightlight in a place where it won't cast a shadow (or no light at all, if possible), and making the elder's bedtime routine a calming experience.

Other physical reasons may exist as to why an elder will stay up later than usual or doesn't sleep through the night. In Lucy's case, before she had her hip replaced, she would get up in the night and try on clothes. Sometimes there would be clothes piled on the floor in huge heaps in the morning. At other times she might pace around her room or wander around the upstairs from bathroom to bedroom, sometimes even coming into the companion's bedroom. Sometimes the companion had to gently get Lucy back into bed three or four times before she would finally go to sleep. It was interesting that this behavior ceased after her hip-replacement surgery and never resurfaced, so it may have been her way of dealing with the discomfort (even though she denied having any pain). Taking notes on what happens before sundowning events may help pinpoint a cause or causes, so the companions can curb the behavior.

Unfortunately, many sleep-aid medications have an adverse effect on persons with dementia, so doctors tend to avoid prescribing them. There may be helpful supplements, but anything given for sleep must be medically vetted and approved by both the medical team and the family. In Lucy's case, she had a naturopathic doctor who prescribed several supplements, including sleep aids. Her primary care provider was fully aware of all of them and oversaw the possibilities of negative interactions with pharmaceuticals. Through this cooperation between medical experts, the care team found a natural sleep aid that kept Lucy sleeping soundly through the night.

Aggressive Behaviors

A behavior that is particularly difficult to deal with in an elder with dementia is aggression. Aggressive behavior can be verbal, physical, or sexual. It is important to consult with a medical provider, because these behaviors can make it difficult to keep an elder in their home, largely because aggressive behaviors make staffing a challenge. These behaviors can occur at any stage of the disease but are more common during the later stages. These behaviors can occur in people who were prone to anger and aggression previously but can also occur in people without this history.

It is important to discern if the aggressive behavior is triggered by pain or discomfort. Elders with dementia might be unable to recognize and express pain or discomfort but still experience the feeling and act out. Another common source of disruptive behavior in elders is a urinary tract infection (UTI). In seniors, UTIs can cause disorientation and behavioral changes. This is true of other infections as well, so if anyone on the care team notices an acute and sudden change in behavior, it is important to seek medical advice for the elder.

Aggressive behavior can also be triggered by frustration on the elder's part or because of a misunderstanding of their companion's intentions or words. Aggressive behaviors can arise because the elder doesn't recognize their companion and, therefore, becomes fearful. Another common cause of aggressive behaviors is hallucinations and delusions, which we covered earlier in this chapter.

Here are some tips to deal with aggressive behavior. With dementia, behavioral issues are often worse in the afternoon and evenings. For this reason, it is helpful to do the activities that cause the most frustration for the elder earlier in the day, for example, bathing. Try to identify what is causing this behavior in the individual. Use distraction and speak to them in a calm and soft manner. It might be helpful to touch the elder lightly on the arm or hand or rub them on their back. If necessary, walk away from any potentially dangerous situation and call for help if needed. Finally, always remember to *not* take this behavior personally, but to report the behavior to the other companions or caregivers and the care manager or family. The care manager or the family can arrange for a consultation with a medical provider, as there might be available treatments.

In Lucy's case severe aggression was not a big problem, as she was an extremely gentle and loving person. However, when irritated, frustrated, or in pain, Lucy did react uncharacteristically with anger and sometimes with some light aggression (swatting). Her doctors prescribed different antidepressants, and she had reactions to all of them. She was also prescribed typical medications to slow the progression of her dementia, and these may have helped a little bit, but the most helpful techniques were distraction and reapproach. The companions would tell Lucy that it was not OK to talk to them in an angry manner, and this would often work, because meanness was not in Lucy's nature. Also, having pieces of art hung or placed around the house that promoted kindness seemed to have a positive effect on her. The companions would also try distraction, but if all else failed, the companions would walk into the next room and come back in a little while and try again.

Sexual Behaviors

An article on www.DailyCaring.com, titled "9 Ways to Cope with Alzheimer's and Sexually Inappropriate Behavior," provides some great methods to better understand and deal with these behaviors. Inappropriate sexual actions can show up suddenly and really take those caring for the elder by surprise. It is important to understand that these behaviors are being caused by brain damage and the disease's effect on the parts of the brain that normally give the elder the ability to control their responses. They may act out this behavior toward their spouse, their children, or their caregivers. The article cites that sexually inappropriate behaviors can be caused by disorientation, being bored, needing physical intimacy, or simply wanting some comfort.

Some other reasons a person with dementia might exhibit inappropriate sexual behavior is they may be uncomfortable in the clothes they are wearing or need to use the toilet. Keeping a log of what is happening at the time of the behavior can help find the reason the elder is acting out. Taking on a more clinical approach than an emotional one can help the companion, family, and friends deal with sexual behaviors more easily. The article on www.DailyCaring.com is a worthwhile read and provides several methods for dealing with this behavior. A few of the suggestions covered in the article are:

- Stay calm and be patient.

- Be gentle but firm and match your body language to your words (frown and shake your head).

- Distract and redirect them to a positive activity.

- If all else fails, shock them by raising your voice and firmly saying, "No!" Look them in the eye to let them know this behavior will not be tolerated.

Some medications have been shown to help, so check with the elder's health provider if other methods for curbing the behavior do not work.

With some dementia patients who exhibit continued inappropriate sexual conduct, a facility may be the only place that can effectively deal with this behavior. Certainly, every effort should be made to try to curb the behavior in the remain-at-home care model, which could even be a more successful option for the elder, as a team of people is honing in on the possible causes and solutions for inappropriate behaviors.

Logging Behaviors Daily

The companions are tasked with entering the events of the day into daily progress notes that are passed along to the care manager or the family (or both). These notes can be tailored to the specifics of a particular elder and what their family or medical team wishes to know. At the very least, changes in behavior, as well as ongoing behaviors that are signs of deteriorating cognition, should be part of the daily progress notes, as they provide vital data to everyone involved in the care of the individual.

We covered other behaviors—sometimes equally challenging—in Chapter 6, such as dealing with bathing, hygiene, and incontinence. These day-to-day care behaviors are more common and can be difficult to manage as well. Companions should record details concerning these behaviors in the daily progress notes.

Despite the trials that can come with caring for a person with dementia, on most days, at least during the early and middle stages, the elder and their companions typically settle into uneventful routines with plenty of enjoyment and contentment.

Addressing Behaviors with Medications

For many of the behaviors described above, doctors can prescribe medications. Unfortunately, many drugs that are commonly used for people exhibiting some of these behaviors, such as aggression or hallucinations, are often avoided for individuals with dementia due to the considerable side effects, which often include further cognitive decline. However, some medications have been specifically developed to delay the progression of cognitive decline and improve unwanted behaviors. The article by the Weill Institute for Neurosciences mentioned earlier in this chapter addresses the usage of medications in great detail for treating the various symptoms that often arise in people with dementia. The article suggests that when a patient's medical team recommends medications, the general advice is to:

- Start at a low dose and then slowly increase the dose based on the patient's response to maximize benefits and minimize side effects.

- Avoid medications that may worsen memory and thinking or increase confusion, since people with cognitive problems may be particularly sensitive to the effects of certain medications.

- Avoid drug interactions that may interfere with medications used to treat cognitive problems.

- Make only one medication change at a time to understand its effects.

Supplements, Diet, and Other Natural Approaches

As with any health condition, what goes into the body ultimately has an effect on the well-being of an individual. Significant research is available on dietary supplements that may aid in fortifying healthy cells to combat the effects of dementia. Positive effects from so-called "brain foods," such as leafy greens, cruciferous vegetables, beans, legumes, MCT (medium-chain triglycerides) oil, fish oil, and lion's mane mushrooms have emerged in some studies, to name just a few.

A plethora of advice exists on how a healthy diet can play a huge role in keeping the body and mind in top shape, including staving off dementia. It behooves the family—and, if possible, the elder as well—to research these options and to always consult with their primary care physician before adding any supplements to the elder's health regimen. (For suggestions on some relevant websites to visit, see the Resources page on our website.)

Living with the Challenges

Elders with dementia should continue going out in public and participating in activities that bring them joy as long as possible. This is one of the key benefits of establishing a team of companions who can support the elder in their home as well as help them participate in various events and outings. On occasion, especially during the latter part of the middle stage and during the advanced stage of dementia, the elder may become disruptive in public (for example, yelling at their companion or becoming defiant). However, the last thing we should do as a society is to hide away our elders simply because they may appear or act a little differently than others around them. Instead, the families and companions of elders with dementia can try the resources and strategies outlined in this chapter to handle many of the disruptions that might occur during the elder's favorite public activities.

As rates of dementia increase with our aging population, hopefully the general public will become more gracious and understanding when a person doesn't quite act in the ways we expect them to. The alternative—keeping our elders almost exclusively in their own homes or facilities—deprives them of many life experiences they should absolutely be enjoying for as long as possible.

Thanks to the Purple Nest Home Care Model, Lucy continued to live a full life up until the final few months of her life when physical challenges suddenly became a part of her everyday world. We may not all be able to "live large," but we can strive to "live full," even while living with the challenges of dementia.

CHAPTER 11
Conclusion

During a visit with Lucy a few weeks before she passed, we—Brynne and Lori—told Lucy about the Purple Nest project that we were working on with Judy. We told her we were basing our business on duplicating the home care model she had received: having the companions live with her in her lovely home and doing their best to make life a full and joyful experience for her, as well as for themselves. We expressed how inspiring she was to us and how much light she carried with her. Lucy had been unable to verbalize what she wanted to say for quite some time, but when we told her about the business, she first smiled broadly, and then she began to cry. And then, to our amazement, she said, "Thank you."

We fully realize that we met Lucy after her dementia had already set in; we never knew her without dementia. For her family and friends who knew her before the disease, the changes in her could be a hard new reality to come to terms with. Our advice though, based on books we've read and our experience with Lucy and other elders with dementia, is that the sooner people can embrace the "new" elder, the sooner they can begin to enjoy the person the elder is becoming.

Throughout the process of writing this handbook and fine-tuning the Purple Nest Home Care Model, time and time again, we have been given signs of affirmation that we are addressing an important subject with the potential to help many people. We share what we have learned through caring for Lucy and others in hopes that, although it may not be the easiest road to take, the Purple Nest Home Care Model can be the road that leads to a better life for people living with dementia, as well as for those who hold them dear.

About the Authors

Lori Kunkel
Co-founder and Managing Director, The Purple Nest

Lori Kunkel brings a deep history of process development and project management to the company. Her project management background was largely in the printing industry where she also developed many training programs to help people navigate complex systems (both computer and task oriented). At the root is her innate ability to grasp the big picture and break down a large project or challenge into simplified, understandable terms. Lori possesses a high level of integrity, inventiveness, and a can-do attitude that has allowed her to hone skills in a variety of niches.

Lori began working as a companion with a woman who had Alzheimer's disease (called Lucy in the Purple Nest handbook), taking care of her in the elder's home. Although Lori had some experience taking care of family members with memory challenges, she had never been a professional companion or caregiver. Those years brought her excellent experience, and she found she really enjoyed the work!

Lucy's family and care team—including Lori—implemented and continually honed the Purple Nest Home Care Model. She was able to build on the model as a companion, with a concentration on creating and maintaining the home as the sanctuary it was meant to be. For instance, Lori organized tasks such as creating an emergency kit, decluttering, and vegetable gardening.

Lori thrives on teamwork and helping others, so joining Lucy's team was a perfect setting for her. She is now bringing this enlightened home care model to many more people who might otherwise have to leave the homes they love and feel safest in.

Judy Schiller
Co-founder and Finance Director, The Purple Nest

Judy Schiller is a former professor and an accomplished organizational development professional with over thirty years' experience in human resources, educational administration, and training. Judy's strengths include increasing individual and team performance through empowerment and improved processes, managing change, and finding creative solutions to challenging problems. Judy is trilingual in English, Spanish, and German after residing in several countries in Europe and Central America.

A multifaceted professional, Judy wears many "hats" in her multiple small businesses, including daily money manager, bookkeeper, trainer, and ceremony celebrant. She has a master's degree in adult education and a bachelor's degree in business administration and German. Judy also has an advanced certification in Interior Alignment, a feng shui school.

Judy initially became involved in Lucy's life in a limited capacity to help with bookkeeping and taxes. Over the years, her role in facilitating positive life changes for Lucy increased exponentially, eventually leading to the creation of the Purple Nest Home Care Model, which offers a higher quality of life for elders with dementia. For this, she refers to Lucy as one of her greatest life teachers! Judy is thrilled to be part of bringing this extremely high-quality model of care to as many people as possible.

Brynne Hicks, MSW, LCSW
Co-founder and Care Manager, The Purple Nest

Brynne Hicks is a licensed clinical social worker and has worked exclusively in the field of geriatric social work. Brynne has a private practice specializing in providing care management for seniors and people under guardianship, including those with dementia, major mental illnesses, brain injuries, and developmental disabilities. Brynne is also a certified professional guardian at both the national and state level.

Through her private practice, Brynne was hired to provide care management for an elder with dementia (called Lucy in the Purple Nest handbook). Brynne managed Lucy's medical care and her caregiving team. As the result of this work, Brynne, Lori, and Judy decided to formalize the Purple Nest Home Care Model. Brynne recognized that Lucy was provided with a reliable staff of dedicated and high-quality companions and caregivers, at a more affordable cost to the family, and that the caregivers had more autonomy than caregivers employed by an agency. It was a win-win-win scenario!

Brynne's expertise in elder care makes her an excellent resource for families embarking on the Purple Nest Home Care Model. She expertly fields all types of questions about how to manage your loved one's complicated medical care; how to hire, train, and supervise companions and caregivers; what to expect from dementia; and how to prepare for the future.

Additional Resources

Need more advice? We're here to help!

Tackling a care solution for an elder can be overwhelming. As you implement the Purple Nest Home Care Model, you may find that you need to customize aspects to best meet the elder's needs (and your family's needs). Or you may need specific guidance to comply with your state's requirements. The Purple Nest team is here to help!

Gain Clarity, Ease Your Stress, and Understand Your Next Steps

Check out our website at www.ThePurpleNest.net to discover:

- **Free resources!**—You will find tips, examples of safety products, book recommendations to learn more, website recommendations to search for team members, and other helpful ideas on the Resources page of our website.

- **Templates, checklists, and more**—We've done the work for you! Visit the Printable Documents page on our website to find detailed, real-world documents you can use right now to implement the Purple Nest Home Care Model. These come free with the purchase of this handbook. To download go to www.mybonuscontent.com or scan the QR code below.

- **Ongoing webinar series**—Join our webinars to learn more about each branch of the model: elder, family, companion, care manager, and daily money manager and much more.

- **Consulting services**—Get trusted advice, creative solutions, and answers to your most challenging questions.

- **Online training programs**—We would love to say that setting up a 24/7 home care model for your elder is easy-peasy, but unfortunately it is not. Take advantage of our online training programs to get educated at your own pace.

Contact us for helpful tools and training, consulting, and speaking opportunities at www.ThePurpleNest.net

www.ingramcontent.com/pod-product-compliance
Lightning Source LLC
Chambersburg PA
CBHW080344170426
43194CB00014B/2680